A LIFE APART
Viewed From The Hills

Jon Boyes and S. Piraban

A work based on interviews with hilltribe people from six tribes in northern Thailand - the Yao, Akha, Lahu, Hmong, Lisu and the Karen. The interviews are arranged in six sections according to tribe and deal with a wide range of subjects from traditional culture to love and sex. An introduction followed by fairly detailed "notes" on hilltribe lifestyles and history precedes the interviews.

SILKWORM BOOKS
1992

ISBN 974-276-568-5
A LIFE APART
Viewed From The Hills
Jon Boyes and S. Piraban

© Jon Boyes and S. Piraban 1989
All rights reserved. No part of this book may be reproduced or transmitted in any from or by any means, electronic or mechanical including photocopying, recording, or by any information storage and .retrieval system, without permission in writing from the publisher.

Cover photographs : Guy Daviot
Cover design, maps : T. Jittidejarak
Photographs: Somporn Aksornskul

Published by
Silkworm Books
35/2 Daokanong Road, Bangkuntien, Bangkok 10150
Tel. (02) 476-5326 Fax 66 (2) 477-1776
Chiang Mai office: Suriwong Book Centre Building
54/1 Sridonchai Road, Chiang Mai 50000
Fax 66 (53) 27-1902
Mailing Address: P.O. Box 76, Chiang Mai 50000
First published September 1989
Reprinted and enlarged 1992

Printed in Thailand by
O.S. Printing House, Bangkok.
Typeset by
Jimmy Printshop Co., Ltd. Chiang Mai.

For my parents - JB.

For A and M - SP.

Acknowledgements

First and foremost we would like to acknowledge our great debt to the many hill tribe people who helped us so much in the preparation of this book. Special thanks are due to Laoair Modagu of Ban Paca Sook Jai, Ja-pu'er Muangjai of Ban Ja-pu'er, Somchai Selee of Ban Kiew Khan (Lahu), and Boonbeng Gangyang of Ban Doi.

Thanks are also due to Pete Boyes for his comments and constructive criticisms, Geoffrey Walton, for doing such a magnificent job editing the original manuscript, and Trasvin Jittidejarak, our publisher, for her constant support and encouragement.

Last but not least we must warmly thank Laogwa Selee, the previous headman of Kiew Khan village, for allowing us two years ago to build a home in his beautiful village, which was, in retrospect, the beginning of everything.

Thai Terms Used In The Text

Farang - The everyday word used by hilltribe people and Thais when referring to a foreigner of European origin. It originally comes from the Thai word "farangset" meaning French.
ban - meaning village.
baht - the Thai unit of currency. There are at present approximately 45 baht to a British pound and 25.50 to an American dollar. (1991)

CONTENTS

INTRODUCTION
- A Life Apart — 1
- Interviews and Methods — 2
- Lifestyles and the Six Tribes — 4

INTERVIEWS

CHAPTER ONE - YAO — 17
1) Life after Mother Passed Away — 19
2) Getting Engaged — 22
3) Lazy Husbands Don't Need to Eat — 27
4) Making Yao Clothes to Sell — 31
5) Affinity of Birthdates, the Lack of — 34
6) Hello Farang! — 37
7) Farming — 39
8) Building a House — 42
9) A Yao Man in Pattaya — 44

CHAPTER TWO - AKHA — 49
1) Spirit Gate — 51
2) Meeting Ground — 54
3) Opium, Prison, and the Seven Japanese — 58
4) Akha Woman — 62
5) Akha Writing and the Dry Cow Skins — 64
6) Ancestors — 65
7) Akha Girl — 67
8) Day School in the Fields — 69
9) New Year — 71

CHAPTER THREE - LAHU 75
1) Refugees 76
2) From Spirits to Christianity 79
3) When the Sky and the Earth Come Together 82
4) Married at Twelve to a Bad Old Man 88
5) Selling Children 93
6) Bird Catching 96
7) Going to Town 99

CHAPTER FOUR - HMONG 101
1) New Village 103
2) Laogwa - Old Headman 105
3) Grandfather-General 108
4) Condoms 112
5) Finding a Bride 115
6) First Love 117
7) Married to a Thai Boy 120
8) Staying Single 123
9) Moving in with the In-Laws 127
10) Little Girl 128
11) School Leaver 130
12) Hunting 134
13) The Spirits of the Boar and Gun 140
14) Hunting Accident 143
15) My Husband - Three Telling Stories 145
16) The First Farang 150
17) Old Woman 152

CHAPTER FIVE - LISU 153
1) Village Patriarch 154
2) The Second World War Comes to the Hills 159

3)	Lisu New Year	162
4)	Buddhist, Not Christian	164
5)	Schoolboy	165
6)	Cow Girl	169
7)	A Woman's Life	170

CHAPTER SIX - KAREN — 175

1)	My Village	176
2)	People Are Changing	178
3)	Dress-Divorce-Death	182
4)	House Spirit	185
5)	Tattoos	189
6)	Going to the Village School	192
7)	An Old Man and his Two Blind Daughters	195
8)	A Strange Village in the Jungle on the Burmese Border	200

EIGHT VILLAGES	203
MAPS	205
RECOMMENDATIONS FOR VISITORS	209
VISITING HILLTRIBE VILLAGES	212
USEFUL PHRASES	216
SOURCES	236

MAP 2: HILL TRIBE MIGRATION ROUTES

INTRODUCTION

Unmistakably individual, with each tribe wearing its own and very distinctive style of dress, farming the mountain slopes that nobody else wants, believers in a thousand and one spirits, independent and proud, humble and hospitable, the tribal peoples of northern Thailand live a life apart.

Originating in the high cold mountains of Tibet and China, these distinct and culturally independent tribal groups have migrated southward in recent centuries, entering a wild, virtually impenetrable mountain region of deep valleys and dense primary jungle. Filtering along the cooler ridge-tops and through the high upland valleys, successive waves of these tribal migrants, fleeing political repression and warfare, or simply looking for new land on which to farm, have gradually spread over the vast area now known as the Golden Triangle, which includes the immense wide plateaus, rugged hills and large upland valleys of Burma's Shan Highlands, the strikingly beautiful sharp mountain ridges of northwestern Laos and the green serpentine ridges of northern Thailand.

In Thailand these southward migrations are halted when mountain ridges give way to lowland plains. It is in the cool hills and isolated upland valleys, away from the hot, crowded plains long since occupied by the ethnic Thais, that the hilltribe people of northern Thailand have made their home.

A Life Apart concerns itself with the six largest of these tribes, who together represent over ninety-five percent of the nation's tribal population of just over five hundred thousand. These are - the Yao, Akha, Lahu, Hmong, Lisu and the Karen. Each of these six tribes has a distinct set of traditions and beliefs, its own language and style of dress. Each tribe is unique and individual, and yet, there being enough similarities in their physical environment and way of life, origin and history of migration, they can be viewed together as a distinct group : the Hill Tribes of Northern Thailand.

We hope that the following sets of interviews with the men, women and children of the hills of northern Thailand will reflect this diversity, whilst at the same time illustrating the hill tribe people's uniqueness in Asian society.

INTERVIEWS - METHODS

The Akha believe in spirits more than many hilltribes, they believe very strongly in spirits. Usually Akha people like to have fun and they think the world is beautiful. They never think about the difficulties of life, never think about being poor.

For us that says it all - an Akha man telling what he thinks about the Akha. The authors would rather hear what Laoair himself has to say about his life and that of his neighbours, than plough through a heavy, fact-filled anthropologist's text-book.

Similarly, for us, a glossy picture book, no matter how stunning the photographs, cannot tell us how, for example, an old Karen man in his younger days went about the winning of his heart's desire by making sure he had the most elaborate tattoos of all the young men in the village. But the old man himself can. And does! This is possible because we are fortunate enough, firstly, to be living in a Hmong village, secondly, to have a very good and often very personal relationship with many hill tribe people, and thirdly, to have enough free time to sit and listen.

And that is exactly what we have done. We have sat and listened and recorded our friends and neighbours, and their friends and neighbours, from six different tribes, gathering together a collection of words, mainly in interview form, which we think illustrate, if not describe, the wide-ranging experiences that contribute to making the hill tribe people and their culture so unique.

Our methods of collecting the interviews were simple. We went to eight villages in Chiang Rai Province over a ten month period in 1988/89. In each village we visited we talked to as many people as we possibly could, men and women, young and old alike, usually in their own homes, but occasionally out and about in the village, or even in the fields.

We did not dictate the subjects, although we did try and suggest general themes. The content and style of the resulting interviews varied considerably. Some were based on events and experiences of a very personal nature, others were explanations of traditional customs and culture. Many were full of humour, some were sad, even heart-wrenching - all were of interest.

Most of the interviews were conducted in Thai, a language that the majority of the hill tribe people speak without difficulty. The translation into English of their words took time, and we trust we have succeeded not only in translating the meaning of their words but also the feelings behind them.

We have tried to keep the editing down to a bare minimum. We have occasionally cut out passages where we feel the speaker has drifted and have sometimes omitted repeated words and phrases where we feel the repetition to be of no significance, and from time to time we have added a word or two to help clarify a particular point. But that is all. We hope we have achieved the right balance.

LIFESTYLES AND THE SIX TRIBES

Broadly speaking the six tribes of this book share a common lifestyle. They are all upland farmers living in village communities, with the family as the most important social unit and the relationship between the human and spirit worlds of vital significance.

1) VILLAGES

Villages tend to be sited at altitudes of over one thousand metres, often on a gentle mountain slope, and can vary in size from less than ten households to well over one hundred. Each tribe builds houses according to its own preference, usually using one of two basic designs - those on the ground, and those elevated on stilts. Materials commonly used are split bamboo and wood planking for the walls and floors, and thatched roofs of grass or large leaves.

2) FAMILY

The family, whether nuclear or extended, is the basis of all social life in a tribal village, and respect for age is of the utmost importance. Normally marriages are within the tribe, with monogamy the norm but polygamy acceptable to all, with the exception of the Karen. The Hmong, Yao, Lisu and Akha are patrilocal, and the Karen and Lahu are matrilocal.

3) VILLAGE LEADERSHIP

Each tribe has a headman whose primary role is to be the representative of the village in all government matters. Some tribes also have a village priest who functions as a ceremonial headman.

4) AGRICULTURE

Slash-and-burn cultivation is the most commonly practised form of agriculture - slash, because it involves the cutting down of all the trees and undergrowth on a wooded hillside, and burn, because once the cut material is thoroughly dried, it is burned off in preparation for planting. Rice and maize are the two most important crops grown. Cash crops planted include coffee, tea, peanuts, soy beans, tobacco and a wide range of fruits. Opium was a favorite cash crop of many of the tribes in the days before tougher government controls.

Domestic animals are kept universally, particularly pigs and chickens which are used extensively as sacrificial offerings in tribal rituals.

The environment is exploited in a variety of other ways. Men hunt and fish and women collect edible plants and raw materials, such as mushrooms, bamboo shoots, roots, nuts, firewood and grass for thatching.

5) DRESS

Most tribespeople are instantly recognisable by the style of their dress. This is particularly true in the case of the women. In general it is the young people of marriageable age who wear the most elaborate clothing. The overall designs of the tribal costumes, whilst retaining their individual distinctiveness, have been changing over the years. In some cases the costumes have been getting more colourful and elaborate as man-made fabrics and ornaments become more readily available. Sewing machines, T-shirts and cheap, factory-made sarongs are becoming more common in the villages.

6) RELIGION

Most of the tribal people are animists, although this simple and much used label does not do justice to the rich and varied beliefs held by the individual tribes. All tribes have a profound belief in spirits and the spirit world. Some spirits, such as household spirits, are friendly and protective, whilst others, such as nature spirits, are either neutral or positively hostile, depending on the circumstances. Ancestor spirits are important and are often called upon to protect family members from harm and illness.

Most tribes have two types of religious specialists; the village priest, who takes charge of the ritual life of the village, and the shaman, who has special powers to communicate with the spirit world.

Buddhism has been widely accepted and Christianity by a small minority.

7) HEALTH

Tribal people have a lower life expectancy than that of the average for Thailand. Poor sanitation, inadequate supplies of clean water, a lack of basic health-care knowledge and poor nutrition all contribute to poor health in the villages.

We try to give the general picture only, as any indepth anthropological examination of the hill tribes would fill many volumes far larger then the present one. We hope the following information, tribe by tribe, will fill in a few details and finally set the scene for the hill tribe people's own words.

YAO

It is thought the Yao, or Mien, as they call themselves, originated in southern China about two thousand years ago. More than a million Yao still live in China, particularly in Hainan, Guangxi and Guangtung provinces. The Yao first entered Thailand towards the middle of the nineteenth century and came almost entirely from Laos.

The majority of the 35,000 Yao in Thailand reside in Chiang Rai, Phayao, Nan and Lampang provinces.

The traditions and dress of the Thai Yao are uniform throughout the provinces they inhabit. Their clothing consists of loose-fitting trousers, which are often highly and intricately embroidered, an ankle-length red-ruffed tunic, a belt and a turban. All garments are black or indigo and are made of cotton cloth.

The Yao speak a Miao-Yao language related to the Sino - Tibetan family of languages. All Yao in Thailand speak a common dialect.

One characteristic peculiar to the Yao is the close affinity of their traditions to those of the Chinese. The Yao have a tradition of writing using Chinese characters which dates back several centuries. Their religion shows a strong Chinese influence in their belief in spirits and the tradition of paying respect to ancestors. The Yao also follow Taoism, a religious belief that has its origin in China. Yao wedding ceremonies also have a very distinctive Chinese flavour and involve the wearing of a special headpiece and ritual garb by the bride, the giving of large dowries, much feasting and drinking and a kowtow cremony in which the bride and groom pay obeisance to the ancestors, the wedding officiators, relatives and guests.

The Yao of all the tribal peoples of Thailand, with the possible exception of the Karen, seem to have the best relationship with the Thais. They avoid open conflict at all times and seek orderliness and perfection in their lives.

AKHA

The Akha, known to the Thais as Ekaw and to the Chinese and Vietnamese as Hani, originated in Yunnan, southwestern China. Many Akha consider the Sipsongpanna region of Yunnan to be their homeland. They have been migrating southward over several centuries, moving into Burma, Thailand, Laos and Vietnam. There are thought to be about half a million Akha still in China and two hundred thousand in Burma. The first Akha entered Thailand from Burma in the early years of this century and initially settled north of the Mae Kok river in Chiang Rai Province.

There are 33,000 Akha now living in Thailand, the majority of whom still live north of the Mae Kok.

In Thailand the Akha can be divided into three main groups according to the style of dress worn. The U Lo-Akha, who have been domiciled in Thailand the longest, wear a pointed headdress; the Loimi-Akha, who are more recent migrants from Burma, wear a flat headdress; and the Phami-Akha, who wear a helmet-like headdress.

The typical dress of an Akha woman consists of a headdress, a hip-length jacket worn over a halter-like garment and embellished on the back by brightly coloured embroidery and applique patterns in red and other colours, a knee-length skirt, a sash and decorated leggings. Buttons, silver coins, beads, feather tassels, gibbon fur, seeds, pompoms, shells and a whole range of other types of ornamentation are used liberally on Akha women's costumes. This is particularly true in the case of the head-dress.

The Akha language falls within the Yi branch of the Tibeto-Burman family of languages. The majority of the Akha in Thailand speak a common dialect.

Of all the tribal peoples in Thailand, the Akha seem to have the highest reverence for their traditions and beliefs. They refer to themselves as the people who "carry the Akha Way." The Akha Way, or Akhazan, covers their religion, their traditions, their ceremonies, the way they cultivate their land, hunt animals and get married, how they treat sickness and death and how they relate to each other and to outsiders. Everything is embraced by the oral traditions of the Akhazan.

LAHU

It is generally thought the Lahu originate from southwestern China and have been moving south into Burma, Laos and Thailand for many years. They are thought to have entered Thailand first from Burma towards the end of the nineteenth century.

Since the Second World War, many more Lahu have entered Thailand having fled from warfare and instability in Burma and Laos.

There are thought to be a quarter of a million Lahu in China, more than 150,000 in Burma and just 10,000 still in Laos. Of the nearly 60,000 Lahu in Thailand, the vast majority live in Chiang Mai and Chiang Rai provinces, with other concentrations being in Mae Hong Son, Tak and Kamphaeng Phet provinces.

The Lahu in Thailand are divided into two main groups-the Black Lahu (Lahu Na) and the Yellow Lahu (Lahu Shi). The Black Lahu are further subdivided into the Lahu Nyi, the Lahu Na and the Lahu Sheh Leh, whilst the Yellow Lahu are subdivided into the Ba Lan and the Ba Keo groups.

Although the different groups of Lahu have different dialects, styles of dress and embroidery techniques, and exhibit variations in settlement pattern and religion, they all show a distinct Lahuness.

Many Lahu groups have given up the daily use of their traditional clothes. This is particularly true of the Christian Lahu Shi. Generally the Lahu Nyi and the Lahu Sheh Leh still wear full traditional dress.

The Lahu language is in the Yi branch of the Tibeto - Burman family of languages. There are five main dialects spoken in Thailand. The Lahu Na dialect is considered to be the standard one and is an important lingua franca for highland peoples in the Lahu areas of Burma, Laos, Thailand and Yunnan.

The Lahu have a history of following messianic movements in China, Burma and Thailand in an effort to counteract economic and political problems. Often these movements have degenerated into armed revolt, leading to further political and economic troubles.

Many Lahu have also turned to Christianity. It is thought that between a quarter and a third of all the Lahu in Thailand live within Christian communities.

HMONG

The Hmong, called Meo or Miao by Thais and Chinese, come from south China. Chinese historical records indicate the Hmong have lived in China's southwestern provinces for well over two thousand years. The Hmong themselves have legends which suggest their ancestors lived in an icy land far to the north, which indicates they may have orginally moved into China from Mongolia, Siberia or Tibet.

For centuries the Hmong have cherished their independence and liberty and for this very reason the Manchus in China first tried to subjugate them. In recent centuries the Hmong fought three long and bitter wars against the Chinese. During this time, many Hmong moved south into Laos and away from China and Chinese persecution. The movement south accelerated after the Hmong's final defeat at the hands of the Chinese in the 1870s.

By the beginning of the twentieth century, many groups of Hmong had reached the northern mountains of Thailand. There are now over 80,000 Hmong in Thailand living in many of the mountainous northern provinces, particularly in Chiang Rai, Chiang Mai, Petchabun and Tak provinces. The majority of the Hmong people, a figure thought to be more than four million, still reside in China.

In Thailand the Hmong are divided into two groups - the Blue Hmong and the White Hmong. The most obvious difference to the casual observer is in dress. Blue Hmong women wear knee-length pleated skirts with batik decoration, and black jackets with a zigzag pattern of embroidery and applique running down the front, whilst the White Hmong women wear loose black trousers and a black jacket with edges and cuffs of blue and, down the front, strips of multi-coloured embroidery. White Hmong women also wear black aprons, edged in blue, with a wide central embroidered panel, and a wide embroidered sash tied at the back with two long pieces of magenta or shocking pink. Blue Hmong women wear a similar but less elaborate apron. White Hmong women wear a black turban and don't like any hair to show, whilst Blue Hmong women usually go hatless and tie their hair in a bun on the crown of their head. All Hmong women like to wear silver jewellery.

The Hmong language comes from the Sino-Tibetan family of languages and is fairly closely related to the language spoken by the Yao people of Thailand. The two sub-groups of Hmong in Thailand speak different dialects.

The Hmong are probably the most widely known hill tribe outside of Thailand. This is a result of recent history in Indo-China. In the 1960s the Hmong in Laos found themselves in the middle of a confrontation between the American-backed Royalists and the Vietnamese-backed Nationalist-Communists, the Pathet Lao. The majority of the Hmong in Laos viewed communism as a threat to their culture and independence and were aligned accordingly, although, partially as a result of

LIFESTLYE AND THE SIX TRIBES • 13

an old clan conflict, many thousands of Hmong did join the Pathet Lao revolutionary movement. A large Hmong army commanded by General Vang Pao, himself a Hmong, which was supported by America, fought throughout the 60s and early 70s. With the victory of the Pathet Lao in 1975, many Hmong left their homes and moved south into Thailand. The majority of these more recent arrivals in Thailand were put into refugee camps along the Thai-Lao border. Some eventually found their way to America and are now living in such widely separated states as Washington and Wisconsin, while others joined the Hmong already resident in Thailand. Many still remain in the camps.

LISU

The Lisu are thought to have originated near the head-waters of the Salween river in China and to have migrated southward into Burma, roughly following the course of the river. The first Lisu entered Thailand from Burma during the opening decade of this century and settled at Doi Chang, near Fang in Chiang Mai Province.

Of the 24,000 Lisu now in Thailand about half live in Chiang Mai Province, with the remainder to be found in the provinces of Chiang Rai, Mae Hong Son, Phayao, Tak, Kamphaeng Phet, Petchabun and Sukhothai.

There are more than 500,000 Lisu still living in China and about 250,000 in Burma, as well as a few thousand in Northeast India. There are no Lisu in Laos or Vietnam.

The Lisu style of dress is not uniform throughout the Lisu areas of Thailand, Burma and China. Generally the clothes worn by the Lisu women in China and Burma are made of hand-woven hemp and tend to be far less bright than the machine-made cotton or synthetic dress of the Thai Lisu.

The Thai Lisu woman wears a blue or green tunic, longer at the back than front, split up the sides, and fastened under the right arm. To the black yoke of this tunic are stitched many brightly coloured bands of cloth. This pattern, which is the distinctive feature of Lisu dress, is repeated on the upper sleeves. The lower sleeves are always red. Knee-length black trousers and red and blue leggings are worn, as well as a wide black sash tied around the waist. Attached to the back of the sash is a pair of tassels consisting of contrasting coloured strands numbering up to two hundred and fifty strands per tassel.

The Lisu language is in the Yi branch of the Tibeto-Burman family of languages and leans heavily on words borrowed from Yunnanese. All the Lisu in Thailand speak a common dialect.

At New Year, Lisu women add to their costume by wearing massive amounts of jewellery. The great lengths to which the Lisu go in making their clothing colourful and elaborate indicates one of the general characteristics of the Lisu - their desire to be the best, to outdo all others.

KAREN

The Karen, called Kariang or Yang by the Thais, are thought to have originated either in Burma or further to the north, possibly in Tibet. They have lived in Burma for many centuries, certainly a long enough time for them to consider Burma their homeland. During the eighteenth century, the Karen first started to move eastwards into Thailand. Since that time, there have been successive waves of migration throughout the later eighteenth, nineteenth and early twentieth centuries.

There are thought to be four million Karen in Burma. Since the nineteenth century, and in particular since the Second World War, a number of Karen have been striving to establish an independent Karen state in the mountains of eastern Burma. The Thai-Burma border is the scene of frequent and bitter fighting between the Karen and Burmese forces.

The Karen are the largest tribal group in Thailand, there being a quarter of a million Karen now living in the country. This figure constitutes over fifty percent of all hill tribe people in Thailand. The vast majority of the Karen are found along the Thai-Burma border from Chiang Rai, Chiang Mai and Mae Hong Son provinces in the north, along the length of the border to the Isthmus of Kra in the south. Scattered groups of Karen can also be found further east.

The Karen in Thailand are divided into two principal groups - the Sgaw Karen and the Pwo Karen. The Sgaw greatly outnumber the Pwo and tend to live more to the north.

Karen women's clothing differs according to whether they are Sgaw or Pwo, mountain dwellers or lowland dwellers, or from the north or south. Generally the women wear sarongs made from two strips of material stitched together to form a narrow tubular skirt, the dominant colour of which is usually red, with added strips of blue, black and gold, and cotton over-blouses of blue, black or indigo, with the lower portions embroidered red and often partially covered in white seed-work. Many variations exist. All unmarried girls and women wear long white cotton shifts. Both Sgaw and Pwo Karen women wear a great variety and quantity of beads and bracelets. They do not wear the quantities of silver generally favoured by other hill tribe women as wealth in Karen society is traditionally invested in livestock and not silver.

The Karen language falls within the Tibeto-Burman family of languages but differs from other members in many aspects and is thus difficult to categorize without qualifiers. There are many Karen languages and dialects in Burma. The two main Karen languages spoken in Thailand, Sgaw and Pwo, are not mutually intelligible.

The Karen are renowned for their weaving skills and in almost every village women and girls can be found busy at their simple back-strap looms producing beautiful garments of woven cloth of the finest quality.

CHAPTER ONE
YAO

1) **Life after Mother Passed Away** - Moey, 23.
   Moey describes how she had to cope with running the household after her mother's death.
2) **Getting Engaged** - Fam-chiang Serdun, 22.
   Fam-chiang explains how young Yao men and women get engaged and what qualities they look for in a prospective partner.
3) **Lazy Husbands Don't Need to Eat** - Fam-hien, 35.
   "Should I work alone? I am not a dog. A man has two hands, two feet." Fam-hien makes her feelings known.
4) **Making Yao Clothes to Sell** - Nai-bu, 21.
   The clothes Nai-bu makes, the costs and time involved and where she sells them.
5) **Affinity of Birthdates - the Lack of** - Nai-bu, 21.
   Nai-bu recounts why her lover's parents labelled her an evil woman.
6) **Hello Farang** - Moi-bu Sewa, 28.
   Some are beautiful, some are not. Some have snake hair and some look like ghosts. Moi-bu describes the westerners she sees walking through her village.
7) **Farming** - Fam-wan Sewa, 52.
   What is grown and when, and why things are getting better.
8) **Building a House** - Chan-wan, 35.
   Chan-wan describes the building of a Yao house.

9) **A Yao Man in Pataya** - Chan-jian, 19.
Chan-jian tells of his work building a hill tribe village for tourists in Pattaya and gives his impressions of the swinging city and its farang visitors.

LIFE AFTER MOTHER PASSED AWAY - Moey

Moey is 23 years old, single, and lives in Ba Rai Luang village. Since her mother's death, she has helped her father and elder brother run the household. She is very skilled at needlework, and to make extra money she embroiders small panels which she sells to a Thai businessman. She works particularly hard in order to be able to help finance her younger brothers' and sister's education. She deeply regrets not having had the opportunity to go to school herself when she was younger.

MOEY: I've never been to school so I'm not good at talking. There was nobody to look after my younger sister. My mother is dead, she died a long time ago. When I was ten years old, I had to look after my younger brothers and sister. I could not work in the fields.

My mother died when she was thirty years old. It was very difficult for me, I was ten years old. I have one elder brother, a little bit older than me. We didn't know anything, we had no idea how to look after my younger brothers and sister. My parents were quite poor, they had little land. I don't know why mother was ill for such a long time. My father told me my mother was ill for many months after she gave birth to my younger sister, the last one, and that she went to sleep under the ground. We never saw her again.

My father started drinking whisky every day. He was upset. My mother was important for the family, very important for the family. After my mother died, we were very poor. My father worked for the local army, the Local Defence Volunteers, but he earned only a little money every month. Our house was very old, full of holes everywhere. When we were young, during the rainy season we used to get flooded inside the house because the water came through the holes in the roof. We had to sit or stand with umbrellas. My elder brother had to go to get banana leaves to make hats for us. We had problems for two years. After that my father started collecting timber to rebuild the house.

INTERVIEWER: Did your mother die at home or in hospital?

MOEY: At first my mother was ill at home for a long time. Then when she got worse my father took her to the hospital. My father and the headman made a stretcher together to carry her to the road. They had to wait for a car to pick up my mother and take her to hospital in Chiang Rai. I didn't go to the hospital. It was during the rainy season and it was very difficult to walk anywhere, especially up and down the hills. My mother was in hospital for a little while. Then she died there. My father and some other people brought my mother's dead body back home. My father didn't tell us our mother was already dead. He told us she was sleeping.

We are five brothers and sisters. I have one elder brother and two younger brothers and one younger sister. Everyone is still single. We work in the fields to get more money for the family. We try to help our father build our new house. It's a very big one. My father tells us that when we have finished the house, he will tell me to get married. He also wants my elder brother to get married. He says my big brother and I will have to look after the house and to look after the younger ones and that everyone must help each other with the work in the fields.

We have a lychee field for everyone in the family to share. My father is quite old and my younger brothers and my sister go to school. I couldn't go to school when I was younger because I had to look after the family. My mother died when my sister was still breast-feeding. I had to buy tinned milk for her. She cried a lot. It was very hard for me after my mother died. Even now it is still very hard, very hard to earn money to pay for my sister and brothers to go to school. I am very sorry I could not go to school. I would like my sister and my brothers to study for as long as they can.

INTERVIEWER: Did your father remarry after your mother died?

MOEY: My father never married again. He had many children. If he had found a new woman, a new mother for me, for us, he would have had to worry that maybe she didn't like the children. I told him to look for a new mother. Sometimes my father was in a strange mood, sometimes getting depressed. I don't know why. But he is a good father. I told him to look for a nice woman to look after him but he didn't want to. He said that no woman could be as good as my mother. He didn't like the idea.

GETTING ENGAGED - Fam-chiang Serdun

> *Fam-chiang is 22 years old and lives with her parents, three sisters and two brothers. Her father is the headman of Lao Shi Guai village and is also the government sponsored village health worker. Fam-chiang helps her mother and sisters run the little village store. She also works in the fields and, as with all Yao women, she devotes a great deal of time to making her embroidered clothes. She is single but is at present keeping her eyes open for a prospective Thai husband.*

INTERVIEWER: Fam-chiang are you married yet?

FAM-CHIANG: No, I have no boyfriend.

INTERVIEWER: At what age do Yao girls usually get married? What is a good age to get married?

FAM-CHIANG: Some Yao girls are twenty-five and still single. But that is quite unusual, really twenty-five is a little bit old. Usually Yao girls get married from seventeen to twenty years. But twenty years old is better, not too old, not too young.

INTERVIEWER: Do the boys and girls choose a partner or do the parents decide?

FAM-CHIANG: It's a free choice. Sometimes two people meet each other for a day, or three days, and if they know they can live together and if they like each other a lot, then they can decide to get married. Some people are friendly and court each other for a year. They have a very good relationship. Some know each other well and get engaged. Most of the men come from different villages.

We meet each other during Yao New Year when boys visit other villages. Boys come to see their relatives in the village. During New Year everybody has to eat in different houses. The boys stay in the village for a few days. It is easy for us to meet them.

During New Year parents give some money to their children to pay for trips outside the village. We usually hire a car to go somewhere for fun. Old people stay at home drinking, eating and playing cards for seven days. We have a very good time.

INTERVIEWER: Can you as a Yao girl marry a man from a different culture?

FAM-CHIANG: Oh, if I want to I can. If we like each other, it is not really important if he is from a different tribe. But most Yao like to marry within the tribe because it is easier to understand each other, with the same language, it is easier to talk together. And anway in a Yao village, we only have a chance to meet Yao men.

INTERVIEWER: After getting married, where do the couple live?

FAM-CHIANG: They have to live with the man's family. A Yao girl before getting married has to get engaged. After getting engaged, she has to stop working in the fields. She has to make clothes for the wedding. They take a long time to make, about a year to finish.

INTERVIEWER: Does the girl have to make the wedding shirt for the man?

FAM-CHIANG: No, as he is a man, his mother has to do it for him. The man has to buy the material for the girl to make her wedding clothes. The girl has to design the clothes herself and do the work.

INTERVIEWER: How do Yao people get engaged?

FAM-CHIANG: The man asks to get engaged. He has to give a dowry in silver to the girl's parents and two silver bracelets to the girl. He gives fifteen ingots of silver to the girl's parents, in Thai money that's about Baht 45,000. This is a low price.

INTERVIEWER: Can the girl ask the man to get married?

FAM-CHIANG: Even if a girl really likes a man, she cannot ask him to get married. The girl has to be shy. But the girl can ask the man to get engaged to her. If a man wants to marry a girl but the girl is not sure about him, she can say yes or no.

INTERVIEWER: When a man wants a wife what does he look for in a girl? Rich? Good-looking? A hard worker?

FAM-CHIANG: Rich or poor is not too important for a man. A good girl, a nice girl and a good worker in the fields and good at sewing and embroidery is important. A little bit good-looking is also important. Some men look only for a good-looking girl. In the end they have problems. To my mind to be only good-looking is not enough. A kind heart is important and being good at work in the fields and a nice girl. It is very unusual for a man to look for only a good-looking girl without considering whether or not she has a kind heart.

INTERVIEWER: When a married couple have an argument, can the woman go back to her family?

FAM-CHIANG: Yes, yes, (laughs) husbands and wives sometimes they have arguments, especially if they have many children and are very busy. Anybody can have an argument. But I don't know why some families have them often. When the woman leaves her husband, she takes the children with her. Sometimes the woman comes from a different village, then every time when she goes away, she takes the children as well.

INTERVIEWER: Does the man have to follow her to ask her to come back?

FAM-CHIANG: Oh yes, (laughs) of course. The man must follow her and ask her to come back. He must be friendly to her.

INTERVIEWER: Can Yao people divorce easily?

FAM-CHIANG: They can divorce but it is very unusual, maybe only two percent do that, because before getting married they have been engaged for one year already. If the man or woman does something bad, they can break off the engagement. If the woman does something bad, then the man can get the dowry back, and the silver bracelets. If a man does something wrong, the woman can break it off and she can keep the dowry. But this never happens. I have never seen it happen.

LAZY HUSBANDS DON'T NEED TO EAT - Fam-hien

Fam-hien is 35, married with children, and now lives in nearby Bong Ba Kaem village. Since first leaving Lao Shi Guai village, she has lived in many places and is therefore considered by neighbours to be experienced and clever.

FAM-HIEN: In eight days time it is Yao New Year so why don't you wait here for the New Year? During Yao New Year we play cards for fun and for money. Can you play cards?

INTERVIEWER: Which day is Yao New Year, Fam-hien?

FAM-HIEN: Yao New Year and Chinese New Year are the same. They start on the same day, on the sixth of February. But on the fourth we have to kill chickens, pigs and ducks. During New Year, we eat in many different houses and drink and play cards for seven days. No work for seven days.

INTERVIEWER: On which day do you stop spending?

FAM-HIEN: Oh, now, even if you stop spending for just one day, it is the same as stopping for ten years. That's difficult. If you stopped spending for one day, you would be rich. Every day we spend money, never stop spending. Even now, I've come here to sit and make clothes, I've been here for only two hours and already my children have come to ask for two baht.

It's very difficult to stop spending, even for half a day. Especially during New Year, you have to give money to the children, much money, in a red envelope. Husbands have to give some money to their wives.

INTERVIEWER: How many children do you have?

FAM-HIEN: How many? (Laughs). I don't want to tell you. Why do you want to know?

INTERVIEWER: Oh Fam-hien, where is your husband? Why did you come to this village? Be careful about your husband, maybe he is looking for a new wife. When he gets a new wife, you will be sorry.

FAM-HIEN: I am nice to him. Uhm, if he wants to, I don't care. Go. I don't mind. I am a woman, I don't worry.

INTERVIEWER: I am joking Fam-hien, I've never met your husband. I'm just trying to get to know you. Now I know a Yao woman is strong and not the same as some of the other hill tribe women. Some women have to work very hard because the men think they have spent a lot of money to marry them. In everything the woman has to obey the man. And the man can be very lazy.

FAM-HIEN: Oh... a lazy man, a lazybones. If he is lazy, he doesn't need to eat. If he doesn't help with the work, he doesn't eat. So, a woman has to work alone? It's not only her business. If a man is too lazy, the family gets very poor. Should I work alone? I am not a dog. A man has two hands, two feet. He has everything the same as a woman. A man is stronger than a woman. For sure I don't agree with those other women. If my husband was lazy, I would not let him eat. He could find his own food.

INTERVIEWER: Before getting married, you can never be sure about your husband. What if he turns out to be lazy?

FAM-HIEN: In the past, a long time ago, the men the same age as my parents were lazy, they didn't like to work. They were bad to the women but the women didn't like to say anything. The men always waited for the women to do the work, to do everything for them. But it is not the same with me. Now it is not the same. If the man is lazy, I have to tell him he doesn't have to eat. Certainly I would want a divorce. A bad man is selfish to the woman. If he is a good man with a nice heart, he isn't selfish. I like a man and a woman to be equal. Some Yao men are lazy, waiting for their wives to work for them, but I don't like it.

INTERVIEWER: Excuse me, what is your family name? How old are you?

FAM-HIEN: You have to know my name? (Laughs). I don't want to tell you. Why do you want to know my name?

NEIGHBOUR: You don't know Fam-hien? They are recording you. Never mind, I'll tell them. Her name is Fam-hien Sejao, she is thirty-five years old.

FAM-HIEN: No, no, ha ha, don't tell her my name. I don't want to talk to them any more.

NEIGHBOUR: Fam-hien they aren't up to anything, they are writing a book about hill tribes, many hill tribes. They are nice people, don't worry about getting a bad reputation.

INTERVIEWER: Fam-hien, if you want, we can take a photograph of you for you to give to your husband. You know, you have a really beautiful face.

FAM-HIEN: Ah, so sorry. Why didn't you come to this village to take a picture of me before when I was younger. Now I am already old. A picture of me now would not be beautiful. No, I don't want it.

MAKING YAO CLOTHES TO SELL - Nai-bu

Nai-bu is 22 years old, single, and has one young daughter. She lives with her parents in Lao Shi Guai village and works in the family's fields. Whenever she is not needed in the fields, she spends all her spare time in making traditional Yao clothes to sell to tourists via a Thai middleman.

INTERVIEWER: Where do you sell the clothes you make?

NAI-BU: When I finish making anything, I take it to Maethao to sell for me. At Bong Ba Kaem village, Maethao's village, there are many farang. The people from this village if they want to sell anything, they take it to Maethao to sell for them. Maethao has many things to sell.

INTERVIEWER: Does Maethao run a hill tribe shop?

NAI-BU: No, Maethao has a small house in Bong Ba Kaem village. She is a very good speaker. The Thai guides like Maethao, they help her to sell things to the farang. She gets good prices.

INTERVIEWER: What do most farang like to buy?

NAI-BU: They like to buy bags. It's easy to sell bags. Bags are useful to tourists.

INTERVIEWER: Do you design or copy the things you make?

NAI-BU: I can't design them myself. I copy the designs from the old things of my mother. I make up a little bit, change the colour and make them bigger. It looks better than the old stuff.

INTERVIEWER: Do you make the material yourself?

NAI-BU: We buy everything from the town. We cannot weave it now. In the past when my parents were younger, they could make the material. Now it is too difficult to do, it is better to buy it, much easier to buy it.

INTERVIEWER: Of all the clothes you make for yourself, what is the most important?

NAI-BU: Four things are important, these are the shirt and the trousers, the turban and the belt. We use these every day. They take a long time to make, about a year to finish.

INTERVIEWER: How much does it cost you to make one pair of trousers?

NAI-BU: A pair of trousers costs about eight hundred baht to make, and takes a long time to finish. Yao clothes take a long time. I have to make everything very neatly. I cannot use a sewing machine. Lisu shirts can be made by machine. Lisu people don't need to think too much when they make their clothes. Lisu clothes only need a little cutting of material, then they are sewn together by machine. If I could make Yao clothes with one, I would use it. Much quicker by machine, it'd save a lot of time.

INTERVIEWER: How many sets of clothes does each person have?

NAI-BU: Not many because they are expensive and take so long to make. One person normally has only two shirts and two trousers. If we have any to spare, we sell them. The money we earn from that we use to buy material for making the next clothes.

If we sell a pair of trousers, we can get fifteen hundred baht, for new ones. If they are a little bit old, then they are cheaper. Most farang like to buy old trousers, second-hand or even third-hand. I don't know why farang like to buy old things. Why don't they like to buy new things that look beautiful and new?

November, December and January, the cool season are the good months for selling. The weather is good for the farang. Every day farang come to this village. After the harvest, we spend our time at home making clothes. It's better than just sitting about doing nothing. But there is not much profit from making clothes to sell. We use the time after we finish eating to make them. Even for five or ten minutes, that's better than doing nothing. But every day we also have to work in the fields.

AFFINITY OF BIRTHDATES - THE LACK OF - Nai-bu

> *Nai-bu's (see Making Yao Clothes To Sell) four year old daughter was fathered by a young man of the village. Nai-bu and her boyfriend had intended to get married but the boyfriend's parents objected on the grounds that Nai-bu's date of birth indicated the relationship would be unlucky. They labelled Nai-bu an "evil woman" and forbade their son to continue the relationship.*

LITTLE GIRL: Mummy, please give me one baht. I am hungry. Hungry, hungry. I want to go home.

INTERVIEWER: She is a pretty little girl. Who is she?

NAI-BU: (Laughing) My daughter.

INTERVIEWER: What? Just now you told me you were not married. Were you joking? Is she really your daughter? Where is your husband?

NAI-BU: Yes, she is my daughter. Her father got married in Padua village at Doi Mae Salong. We separated a long time ago. Something came up so we couldn't live together. We were unlucky.

INTERVIEWER: What happened? Why were you unlucky?

NAI-BU: He used to live in this village, but his parents moved to Padua. They took him with them. Now he has married a Yao girl in Padua. The reason we could not live together before was that our birth dates did not match. It would have been unlucky to marry. Maybe he or I would have died if we'd got married. His parents worried about that. They took him to live with them at Padua. I am sorry for my daughter. When we separated, my daughter was one. Now she is four years old.

INTERVIEWER: For Yao people if you have children and separate, does the woman look after the children or does the man help? Who leaves the house?

NAI-BU: For Yao people if you separate, the man has to get out. The woman can keep the house and the children. Me and him, we didn't argue, we had no problem together. His parents worried about him too much. They didn't want us to marry. We really loved each other. I loved him and he loved me. We were good friends.

His parents didn't like me. They thought I was an evil woman because my birth date is stronger than his. They said we could not live together. His parents believe in spirits, but I don't. I have seen some couples who have bad birth dates, the wife is called an evil woman, but they live together and get rich, they have no problems. I think for some people the birth dates are not too important. They marry, they live together until they die.

He is a nice man. Before, he came to see my daughter. Sometimes he gave some money. Now he is married and too busy to come. I understand. Sometimes I see him at Mae Chan market, he buys something for my daughter. I often go to the market to sell maize and beans, and sometimes I go shopping there.

INTERVIEWER: Now you are twenty-two, it is not too late to marry again.

NAI-BU: Oh I don't know, I am not sure. If I meet a good person, I would like to marry. For a hill tribe person, like for anyone, it is difficult to live alone. You need someone to help you work in the fields. If I had a husband to help me work, the family would get richer and have a better life.

INTERVIEWER: When you lived together, did he help you with the work in the fields?

NAI-BU: Oh, before we weren't married, we didn't live in the same house. We had to separate. At the beginning, his parents liked me a lot. I don't understand many things in this world.

HELLO FARANG - Moi-bu Sewa

Moi-bu is 28 years old, married, and has two children. She has lived in Lao Shi Guai for most of her life. Her house fronts the small dirt track that runs through the village and so she has ample opportunity to watch the various people passing through - including the rather strange farang.

MOI-BU: I have lived in this village since before the present houses were built, about eighteen years now. Before we had another village across the bridge.

In the past there were no farang. But in the last few years, farang have been coming to this village. Now they come nearly every day. Most farang are alright, we have no problems with them. It is good if they come to this village because I can sell embroidery.

Some farang are very beautiful, some farang are not beautiful. The same as Thai people, some are beautiful, some are not. Farang women have an ugly way of walking. Most farang women walk like men, they have big legs. Some farang girls are very beautiful, beautiful the same as Thai beauticians. Some farang girls with small bodies are beautiful like Miss Thailand.

I have seen some farang who have hair like snakes, hundreds of snakes. They make it look like snakes. It looks frightening. Yesterday I saw a farang man who had snake hair. He walked past my house. The children ran away, they were frightened. The children are also frightened of the black people, the black people with curly hair. I have heard that black farang eat children. Some farang look like ghosts, they cut their hair in strange ways.

I think farang have good hearts. The people in this village have never had problems with farang. Sometimes they drink whisky but they are very quiet, very polite. Whether they drink a lot or a little bit, it is difficult to know, difficult to know if they are drunk or not. I think farang have better hearts than Thais.

Sometimes the children cry, they are frightened of farang. The farang then try to play with the children, to make the children feel better. Then the children are not frightened of the farang. Most people prefer farang to Thai. I don't know why. When farang come to the village, the children or the people like to say, "Hello farang". But for Thai people, they don't say anything.

FARMING - Fam-wan Sewa

Fam-wan is 52 years old and is a minor wife to her husband. She and the principal wife have a good relationship and spend a lot of their time working together about the house. She has three children, the eldest of whom works for the local government in the agriculture department.

FAM-WAN: My daughter knows about farming but she is not here today. My daughter goes to college on Saturdays and Sundays. She works for the people in the village. My daughter has been to agricultural college. She worked in Lampang Province and Mae Hong Son for two years. She knows many things. She used to work with farang.

INTERVIEWER: Can you tell me what crops you grow?

FAM-WAN: I am happy to tell you. Now the people in this village have a better life. Most people grow mountain rice and paddy rice in the rainy season. When we finish the harvest, I mean the paddy rice harvest, we plant beans and peanuts. Some people plant cucumber and vegetables and garlic and many other different things. But the crops where they can make money are peanuts and soya beans. They can make big money.

In June and July we prepare the soil. Then in early August, the rains start and the people begin to plant rice for the family to eat. If they want to grow corn, they plant it at nearly the same time. After that, they have to look after the fields until the harvest. They have to cut the grass and weeds. If you keep cutting the grass, the crop grows very quickly and very well. You have to keep weeding the fields until November when the corn and the paddy rice and mountain rice can be harvested.

When the rice and corn harvest is finished, we start to plant soya beans and peanuts. We are able to plant paddy rice twice a year. The first time we call it *tam na bee* and the second time we call it *tam na blang*.

In a year, my family can grow many things. The mountain rice crop is for the family. But we make money with paddy rice, corn, soya beans and peanuts. We make a lot of money with peanuts. But we have still another crop for the family for the future when we can make really big money. It is lychee and takes three years before it can be harvested. Now we have to look after our two lychee fields using chemicals and insecticide. We get no fruit the first three years. Then after they start to flower, they give fruit. This is the important time so we have to spray them with insecticide to stop the insects coming to eat the blossoms and the very young fruit. We have to spray every week. When the fruit gets a little bit bigger, we tie paper bags over each bunch of fruit to protect them from the sun and the birds.

INTERVIEWER: How much money do you make in a year?

FAM-WAN: I am not sure, but compared with the years before, it is much better. The people in this village, everybody, has a better life. They eat well, they are not hard up any more. You can see from the clothes. They eat well. They have a good life.

INTERVIEWER: You grow and sell corn, rice, beans, peanuts and vegetables. Do you get anything from the forest to sell?

FAM-WAN: Er, I have to think. Yes, we get grass from the forest to make brooms. We sell the grass for about six or seven baht a kilo. That's not much.

Everything is getting a lot better because of my daughter. She knows all about how to use chemicals. Everybody in our village can work all year round to make money.

BUILDING A HOUSE - Chan-wan

Chan-wan is 35 years old, married, and has four children. He hires out as a day labourer to work in his neighbours' fields or to help with building work in the village. His neighbours consider him good-looking and call him a bit of a playboy.

INTERVIEWER: What do you do before you start to build a house?

CHAN-WAN: People who want to build a house have to cut a lot of timber and bamboo, get nails, big and small and make the grass panels for the roof. You also have to get the timber for making the bedrooms. This is for a simple house, a Yao or Hmong style house. It's very easy. Then you have to make the ground flat and dig holes for the main posts. You have to ask your neighbours and everyone in the village to help with the building.

INTERVIEWER: What do the women do?

CHAN-WAN: The women have to cook. Some women help to carry the planks and help to thatch the roof panels. The people first plan how big the house is to be, how many posts are needed, how many bedrooms, where to put the front door and where the back door will be. Then they put up the main posts for the house, sometimes eight. After that you make the bedrooms you want. You have to build the inside walls of the bedrooms, often three bedrooms. In the main room you have the cooking place and a sleeping platform for children or guests. Then you make the doors for the bedrooms. In the bedrooms you have a wooden floor, not dirt.

When you have built the walls and the roof and finished the doors and the bedroom walls, you make the cooking place. You mix dirt with water to get clay and build a low wall, quite thick. You have to wait three days for it to dry out. Then you put the big cooking pan on the top. Now everything is done.

In the past, a long time ago, they used to sacrifice to the spirits and they had to check the day before building. They had to find out which day was an auspicious one for building a house. They also used to get the auspicious time to start the building. Now they do not do anything for the spirits but they still choose the day in the same way.

One thing is important, that is the building of the cooking places. One place is for cooking food and the other for boiling vegetables for fodder for pigs and other animals.

Hill people's houses are easy to build, simple, and not much money is needed to build one. You only have to buy nails and some of the wood. You don't have to spend anything on labour. When the house is finished, you celebrate moving into the new house by drinking whisky and eating chicken or pork.

A YAO MAN IN PATTAYA - Chan-jian

Chan-jian is 19 and single. He has left Lao Shi Guai to work in Pattaya on a project to construct an "authentic-looking" hilltribe village for tourists. We interviewed him when he was back in the village for his elder brother's wedding.

CHAN-JIAN: I have been working in Pattaya for over a month. Miss Noi came to this village to ask people to work in Pattaya. Miss Noi is in business. She works for two men who come from Mae Chan. She went around asking many hill tribe people to go to build a hill tribe village in Pattaya.

INTERVIEWER: Is this the first time you've been away from the village?

CHAN-JIAN: I've never been anywhere on a holiday trip. Never, never, but I went to work in Bangkok before. I was a carpenter. In Bangkok it was too hot for me, terrible weather. I like Bangkok but I don't like the weather. I like the city but I could not live there. I had to come back home. My village is not hot. In Bangkok I used to shower four times a day. I worked there for a month.

INTERVIEWER: Did you have any problems working in the city? Did you have an identity card?

CHAN-JIAN: That was no problem for me, only the heat. I had an I.D. card.

INTERVIEWER: How different is Pattaya from a small Yao village?

CHAN-JIAN: Oh, there's a big difference. It is a pity I have not studied, really a pity. In Pattaya there are many farang in the shops, in the bars, in the supermarkets; only farang. Many farang are with Thai women. Then the prices in Pattaya are very, very expensive. The food is very expensive, but it is the best. If you buy food and cook it yourself, it is a little bit cheaper. While I have been living in Pattaya, I have got thin. If I eat too much, I spend too much. At the place where I work there is food for everyone, but sometimes I don't want to eat it. It is good food but nothing special. It is not the same as at my house in my village. Here I can eat at any time. I don't have to buy rice or vegetables. I can eat a lot. But the whisky in Pattaya is not too expensive, but still a little bit more expensive than in Chiang Rai.

I earn fifteen hundred baht a month and I get free food and accommodation. It is still not enough. I earn fifteen hundred baht but if I want to go somewhere I have to pay for transport. But I am happy anyway.

I want to work in the future so I try and practise speaking English. If I can speak English, I can get a better job and earn more money. At my job the work is good, there is not much to do. Early in the morning, I water the garden. Sometimes I help to build the houses. I look forward to being a hotel doorman later.

INTERVIEWER: What other hill tribe people are working with you in Pattaya?

CHAN-JIAN: Yao, Karen, Meo, Akha, Lisu and Lahu. All the tribes live in one village, close together but in separate houses. They do not live together. The Yao people build the Yao style houses, the Akha people build the Akha style houses, Lisu, the Lisu houses, Lahu, the Lahu houses and Karen, the Karen style houses. The Yao and the Meo houses are nearly the same design.

Everyone has a good life, they enjoy living there. They live there like in their own village. They have their own stuff for cooking, but some things the manager gives them. The women do embroidery to sell and the girls work, sometimes they dance as a show for the tourists, sometimes they play games, sometimes they sing for the tourists. They do many different types of dancing: Yao; Akha; Lisu; Karen; Lahu. They put on shows for the farang tourists.

When farang come to see the place, they have to pay. For dancing, a girl sometimes gets thirty baht, sometimes fifty baht. If a farang takes a photograph, he has to pay five baht. It's five baht for every picture they take. The money they pay for taking pictures goes into a box. Every month we share the money out between everyone in the village. If the women sell embroidery, they can keep the money themselves.

Now it is not too easy to sell the embroidery because we are still building. There are not many farang yet, but the manager already has a plan to build a big restaurant and a car park.

INTERVIEWER: Do you enjoy living in Pattaya? Do you have fun?

CHAN-JIAN: Pattaya is different from here at home. Fun in Pattaya comes from spending money, eating and sometimes going to a bar. If I have a lot of money, I have plenty of fun. If there's no money, there's no fun. I have to worry about getting enough to eat. I have to eat every day.

It is not the same in my village. Here I can have natural fun. Without money I can still enjoy myself. I can go off in the jungle, shooting birds, walking up in the hills, and looking after the cows. Fun. Even with no money I can have it, but it's a different sort of fun.

In Pattaya when it gets dark there are lights everywhere. It is very light, everywhere coloured lights - in the trees, in the lanes. The coloured lights are very beautiful. I think Bangkok is not so beautiful.

I think the farang in Pattaya are proud. They are not interested in looking at the village, or walking. Many farang are big, they look very clean but they don't look strong. I think they are interested in women. There are so many bars. There are many women in Pattaya, they wear ugly clothes, sometimes only a bra and very small pants. I don't know why they like to wear them. Me, I look many times, they are so ugly, not pretty, not beautiful. They want to show their bodies to the farang. I don't like it but sometimes I like to have a quick look. I think every man likes to have a secret look.

I don't think Pattaya is in Thailand. I think Pattaya must be somewhere in a farang country. I like the farang who come to see the small villages like my own. They are friendly, they like to talk to the people. The ones who come to my village like to walk. They don't mind if it is a little bit dirty. I prefer the farang that walk to my village, I like them a lot. I don't like the farang in Pattaya.

CHAPTER TWO
AKHA

1) **Spirit Gate** - Laoair, 28.
   Laoair describes how and why the spirit gate is built.
2) **Meeting-Ground** - Laoair, 28.
   A place for boys and girls to get to know each other, for old people to sit and talk and for children to play and have fun. Laoair dispels some false assumptions.
3) **Opium, Prison, and the Seven Japanese** - Laoair, 28.
   Laoair explains how, through his going to prison and learning to speak good Thai, he earned himself a free trip to Japan.
4) **Akha Woman** - Boo-se, 73.
   Boo-se describes how she first met her husband.
5) **Akha Writing and the Dry Cow Skins** - Laoair, 38.
   The explanation for there being no Akha writing today.
6) **Ancestors** - O-Lokar, 62.
   O-Lokar tells of the birth of the Akha people and of Ooma-um-kwang, the very first Akha women to become pregnant.
7) **Akha Girl** - Amiyo, 12.
   Amiyo describes her work in the fields and her efforts at making her Akha clothes.
8) **Day School in the Fields** - Meesia, 15.
   Meesia tells of how the village teachers follow the children to the fields to carry on the teaching.

9) **New Year** - Laoair, 28.
   Laoair describes in detail the rituals and day-by-day events of the Akha's two New Year celebrations.

SPIRIT-GATE - Laoair

Laoair is 28 years old and is married with no children. He lives with his young wife in a small, light, airy house, built of bamboo and thatched grass and elevated on stilts - a house typical of Paca Sook Jai village. Laoair is a keen hunter.

INTERVIEWER: Laoair, when do the people in the village have to build a new gate again? How do you build the gate?

LAOAIR: Er, the *Law-kah* we build every year. Every year before we build the gate, the spirit-man takes rice soup, local corn whisky, ginger-juice and fresh water, a bamboo water container, eggs and rice and offers them to the spirits of the very old ancestors. After that everybody has to work together to build the gate. Some people dig the holes for the two posts - three metres apart and three metres high. Other people make the carvings to put on the gate, on the cross-beam. At the two ends we make a man's and a woman's face, one at each end.

We have many different carvings on the gate, many animals, birds, helicopters, and M-16 guns. They are all painted red. Next to the two posts, we put wooden carvings of a girl and a boy making love. One couple on each side. Nearby the figures of the couples making love, there are baskets and spice containers, and many other things from everyday life.

We build everything to explain about the people, about their lives, and about making love and working, and to separate the bad spirits - to stop them coming into the village - from the good spirits. We Akha people believe that everything on the gate helps to stop bad things from coming to the village.

INTERVIEWER: Where in the village can you build the gate?

LAOAIR: The spirit-gate must be built a little bit away from the village, but before you get into the forest. When many people are ill in the village, we have to change the place for the gate. But not when people get normal illnesses, only when many people are getting unusual ones. We also have to change the place for the gate if bad things like house-fires or crop failures happen. The headman decides whether or not we have to build a new gate at a different place. If things are really bad, we have to move the whole village.

INTERVIEWER: I have seen some Akha villages that do not have a gate. Why don't they have a gate?

LAOAIR: Every Akha village, if they believe in the traditional Akha culture, will have a spirit-gate. The spirit-gate is a very important thing, nobody can touch it for a whole year. If somebody does not know, and they touch it, then they have to supply a pig to appease the spirits of the gate. And the spirit-man will have to make the offerings again, but this time just the pig.

The spirit-gate embraces the people the same as parents do their children.

When building the gate, nobody can take off their shirts or roll up their trousers. Everybody must be well dressed. They must be respectable. If somebody ignores this and comes to the gate without a shirt on, he has to pay for a pig to be sacrificed.

MEETING-GROUND - Laoair

> *Laoair (see Spirit-Gate) has had three previous wives, and is now thinking of divorcing his current, very pretty and hard-working wife, and marrying for a fifth time. He has already found the girl he intends to wed. None of his wives have yet given him a child, thus he feels he must keep changing partners until one eventually bears him an offspring. His good looks and keen sense of fun help him in attracting new brides.*

INTERVIEWER: How do Akha people get married?

LAOAIR: Akha boys and girls marry if they talk it over and agree to be husband and wife. But they also have to ask their parents. If their parents agree, then the man gives a bottle of whisky and one old silver coin to the girl's parents. The girl has to bring her clothes and all her belongings and move into the man's house. The man kills a pig and a chicken and gives eggs to the spirits. After that they have a celebration. If the man is rich, he buys many bottles of whisky, sometimes one or two hundred bottles. Men and women, everyone, has to drink. They have a big celebration. All the old people in the village are invited to come and eat and drink first.

INTERVIEWER: How do boys and girls meet each other before they get married?

LAOAIR: In the village we have a meeting place, here the girls and boys meet each other and flirt. We call this place *laan-der-hong*.

INTERVIEWER: I have heard about the *laan-sao-gawt*, but not the *laan-der-hong*. What is the difference? Can you explain?

LAOAIR: I want to explain everything clearly. Really we do not call it *laan-sao-gawt*, we call it *laan-der-hong*. *Der-hong* means "a place to visit." It means the place to visit or the place to meet each other. *Laan-sao-gawt* is a new word used by Thais. Some Thais come to the *laan-der-hong* to watch Akha girls and boys embrace. Thais think it is the place to embrace girls. So, they call it the place to embrace girls, *laan-sao-gawt*. They have misunderstood.

Really for Akha people the place is a nice place for the village people. It is a place where anyone can go and meet other people, to talk, to flirt. But Thais think it is just to embrace, so they call it by the wrong name, with a wrong meaning. Some Thai people think it is the place to embrace and that anybody can be embraced. They think it is the place for sex. They think anybody can go there and make love, and do whatever they want to do. They are wrong.

INTERVIEWER: When did you build the meeting-place?

LAOAIR: We built it a long time ago, at the same time we first built the village. We came from Burma. In the past the ancestors said that most Akha people work hard in the fields and get tired, but when it gets dark there is nowhere for them to go. They said we must have a special place. Living in an Akha village is not the same as living in the town where there is electricity. All Akha people get tired. After dinner we must have somewhere to sit, to meet, to talk, and a place for boys and girls to meet each other and be friendly together, and also a place where children can be away from the old people and play together. The ***der-hong*** is the place. Our ancestors had the same. It is a good place to sit and talk after dinner. It is the place where people can fall in love. We believe we must give time to young people to be friendly together. They need time to decide whether or not to be husband or wife. They have a good opportunity at the ***der-hong***. But the young people don't decide alone, they still have to ask their parents.

INTERVIEWER: What are the important considerations before deciding to get married?

LAOAIR: The girl and the boy who want to get married have to be good workers in the fields. They have to realise how difficult it is to work in the fields, and they mustn't be lazy.

INTERVIEWER: How do they court each other?

LAOAIR: They sing songs about how difficult it is to work in the fields, about nature, and about the person they like very much. They come to meet each other especially when it is lovely weather, when there is no rain, and when there is a moon. Everybody has fun.

They often sing in harmony, it's very nice to hear, the voices go all over the mountains. And often they dance and clap hands together. It's really lovely.

Some girls and boys like each other very much, they will get married. Sometimes they show their affection by embracing in public.

At the same time at the meeting-place, older people sit and talk about working and hunting, about looking for food and about the family. The children play and have fun.

INTERVIEWER: In many cultures if an unmarried girl holds hands with a boy, or embraces a boy, the house-spirit will bring the girl bad luck.

LAOAIR: For the Akha, there is nothing wrong with holding hands or embracing, or kissing, or even making love before getting married. Akha girls know Akha culture, they know what they are doing. They cannot make love with just anybody, like an animal. A girl must love the boy to whom she gives her heart and body, love him a lot.

INTERVIEWER: What happens if she doesn't like the boy who holds her hand and embraces her?

LAOAIR: If she doesn't like the boy, then he cannot do anything with her. Some Thai men come to the meeting-place in the hope that they can embrace any Akha girl, and make love to any girl. But they cannot do it, because Akha girls are not interested in a man from a different culture.

OPIUM, PRISON, AND THE SEVEN JAPANESE - Laoair

Laoair's (see Spirit-Gate/Meeting-Ground) village lies near the Chinese nationalist refugee town of Mae Salong, at one time an important centre of the drug trade in northern Thailand. Many local people, Chinese, Shan and hill tribe, were at one time or another involved in the growing or selling of opium. Laoair dabbled in both and was eventually caught and sentenced to three years imprisonment.

INTERVIEWER: How many people still smoke opium in your village?

LAOAIR: Now in our village not many people smoke opium, usually only the old people smoke. Young people don't like to smoke. Government officials and the headman try to stop people growing opium. The officials teach the villagers to grow vegetables, any kind of vegetables. They don't like us to grow opium. Now it is difficult to get opium in the village.

Not many people smoke. In the past some missionaries came to the village and told the people to stop smoking, even to stop smoking cigarettes. We believe in spirits, but some families became Christian.

INTERVIEWER: You speak good Thai, perfect Thai, where did you learn to speak such good Thai?

LAOAIR: Oh, I don't like to say, I'm too embarrassed, but... well, in the past I used to sell opium to the people in the village. Then one day the police came and caught me. I was sentenced to three years in prison. I learnt Thai in prison. I also started to learn the Thai alphabet in prison.

INTERVIEWER: Could you speak any Thai before you went to prison?

LAOAIR: No, I couldn't, not at first, I couldn't even count, one, two, three. I still remember the first day. I heard someone say, "Today we have to welcome our new brother." I could understand just a very little Thai. I was very glad to hear the words, "welcome new brother." For the Akha, the word welcome means people give everything free, it means there is good food, and everybody has to be friendly. But welcome in the prison means fighting. Everyone in the prison fought me. They boxed me Thai style. I was very scared. Many people punched and kicked me. I had no chance to hit back. I thought it was my last minute.

I lost consciousness. When I came to, I felt very bad. All my body ached and I was very wet. But they helped me. They picked me up. Some gave me cigarettes, some gave me something to eat. Everybody was friendly to me. I felt much better then, but better only in my head, not my body.

INTERVIEWER: Did your parents and your wife visit you in the prison?

LAOAIR: My wife came sometimes. I have no parents, they died when I was very young. My wife came to see me and brought cigarettes and soap for me. I felt sorry for my wife. I told her, as I had to stay in prison for three years, she could marry a new husband if it was difficult for her to work alone. I told her I didn't mind. But I was a little bit upset when she did marry again. Three years is not really a long time. She wasn't my first wife. My first wife and I separated before I was caught selling opium.

I've had three wives altogether. I separated from my first wife because she couldn't get pregnant. She had no children. None of my three wives had any children. I want to have a child. If a wife cannot get pregnant, then I have to look for another one. I am very sorry that I have no children. I have been taking herbal medicine. I have tried many things, but I still can't get them pregnant. When I went to Japan, the Japanese people took me to see a doctor, a Japanese doctor. He told me I could not make my wife pregnant.

INTERVIEWER: Japan? You went to Japan? How did you get the chance to go to Japan?

LAOAIR: I was very lucky. After three years in prison I could speak very good Thai. One day some Japanese tourists came to visit my village. There were seven of them. One of them could speak quite good Thai. I enjoyed talking to them. They wanted me to take them to see the opium fields. So I took them. After showing them the fields, I took them trekking in the jungle for two days. Everybody was happy. They made a video film. After seeing the fields and the jungle, the seven Japanese came to stay in my house for three nights. They offered to take me to visit Japan. I thought they were joking. Surely nobody wants to spend thousands of baht just so I can go to Japan. So I said to them, "O.K. I'll go to Japan."

After that the Japanese people arranged everything for me. They got me a passport and did all the paperwork and took me straight to Bangkok to buy the ticket. They also gave me some money. Then they took me to Japan, altogether for forty-three days. I had a lot of fun.

INTERVIEWER: Did you ever feel uncomfortable? Did you get angry or frustrated with anything?

LAOAIR: No, no, I didn't get angry. If I was angry, then I was angry with myself, angry that I was too stupid to be able to speak English or Japanese. It was difficult to communicate, but I had a lot of fun. In Japan everybody was good to me. I went to many places, but I don't know where exactly, as I can't read Japanese. They took me to eat in very good restaurants. I had never in my life eaten such good food.

They will come to see me again next year.

AKHA WOMAN - Boo-se

Boo-se is 73 years old, married with two daughters, and lives in Mai Paca village. She spends most of her time looking after her husband and her grandchildren. She no longer works in the fields but does go to them fairly regularly to collect vegetables for the family's consumption.

INTERVIEWER: Where did you meet your husband? Can you tell me about your life when you were younger?

BOO-SE: Ohh, I cannot speak good Thai, I hope I can speak enough for you to understand me. I was married when I was nineteen years old. I have two daughters. My eldest daughter married an Akha man from the village. The younger daughter married a man from Phrae Province, a Thai man. They live in Phrae. Sometimes they come to see me. They always bring something for their father and mother. Usually it is something to eat, like fish, or sometimes salt or tobacco. My daughter wants to come back to live with her parents, but my son-in-law doesn't want to. In the mountains it is very difficult to make money, there's not enough money here for him

INTERVIEWER: Where did you meet your husband? Did you both come from the same village?

BOO-SE: Yes, we came from the same village. We met each other at the meeting-place. Porthao courted me the whole night until the early hours. In the morning I went back to my house and did the cooking, ate, and then went to the fields. We were being friendly together for many days.

One day he asked me to spend the night with him on top of the rice store next to my parent's house. Then we made love. But we had already agreed that we would marry. He promised me he wanted to marry me.

INTERVIEWER: Were your parents angry that you made love on the rice store?

BOO-SE: No, no, my parents did not know that we made love. If they had known, they would have been angry.

INTERVIEWER: What are the Akha men like after they've got married?

BOO-SE: My husband is a little bit different from the other Akha men. He helped me to do everything. We worked together, we went to the fields together, we threshed rice together early in the morning. We did everything together. Even now, he still helps me.

AKHA WRITING AND THE DRY COW SKINS
- Laoair

Laoair of Mai Paca village is 38 years old and single. He is the younger brother of O-Lokar, the headman, (see Ancestors) whom he lives with and helps in his duties as headman.

INTERVIEWER: Do the Akha have a written language and an Akha alphabet? I have never seen any Akha writing.

LAOAIR: We have an old story about it. In the past we had an Akha alphabet. They used to write on 'dry-cow-skins.' When they had to move the village, they had to carry all the cow-skins. The skins were very heavy and difficult to carry.

Then the headman had an idea how they could make it easier to carry all the skins. They decided to cook the skins with the Akha writing on them and eat them. Everybody would eat the 'dry-cow-skins.' The Akha people thought that the Akha writing, the alphabet, would still be in the body. Everybody agreed and they cooked the skins and ate them.

After that, the Akha writing was gone from that time till now. Nobody knows how to write Akha anymore.

ANCESTORS - O-Lokar

O-Lokar is 62 years old and is the headman of Mai Paca village. His father was the headman before him, and his son will the headman after him. His family name is of great significance to the Akha as it is the name of one of the original nine spirits in Akha mythology.

INTERVIEWER: How long ago did you build the village here?

O-LOKAR: About twenty-five years ago. We separated from Abe village.

INTERVIEWER: How many headman and spirit-men have you had in that time?

O-LOKAR: For twenty-five years it has only been men from my family who have been the headmen. In the past my father was the headman and the spirit-man. After my father died, the people chose me to be the headman.

INTERVIEWER: Can the people in the village choose anybody to be the headman?

O-LOKAR: They choose the same family to be headman again and again. In Akha culture we believe that male ancestors are important, and also one or two women ancestors. My family name, O-Lokar, is very important. We are from the past, we are from a long, long time ago.

INTERVIEWER: Where do the Akha ancestors come from?

O-LOKAR: The first Akha ancestors come from Burma. Very old people told us that the first Akha person was Ooma-um-kwang. She was the first Akha woman to become pregnant. She had a girl whose name was Sm-mi-o. This woman, the number two woman, is very important. It is she who gave the names to all Akha people.

Ooma-um-kwang and Sm-mi-o are very important for all Akha people. We also believe in nine spirits who died a long time ago, but now I have forgotten their names.

Now there are many different Akha family names. The first word of the name is taken from the last word of the name from the person before.

The Akha think that the Akha, the Chinese, the Japanese and the Lahu came from the same place and separated later. But we are not sure.

AKHA GIRL - Amiyo

Amiyo is 12 years old and lives in Paca Sook Jai village. She works every day in the fields with her mother and elder sister. She is just beginning to learn the various methods involved in making her own Akha outfit. At present she wears the less elaborate clothing of a young girl.

INTERVIEWER: Amiyo, do you work in the fields every day?

AMIYO: Mmm.

INTERVIEWER: You work every day?

AMIYO: I never have a day off, except during New Year. I have to come to the fields every day with my mother and sister to work. In my family there is only my mother, my sister, and me who can work.

INTERVIEWER: What does your father do?

AMIYO: My father is already old. He looks after the house, and the pigs, chickens and horses. He boils food for the pigs and he cooks for my mother. My father has to do the woman's work. He has to thresh the rice, we have no machine.

We have to work in the fields. We have to clear the land, burn the stubble and dig the soil. Then we leave it, waiting for the rain. We work slowly. Sometimes many friends come to help.

We bring rice to the fields to eat. When we stop for lunch, my mother and my sister usually do some sewing. This year my elder sister becomes a woman, ha ha, she has to make her own clothes. Sometimes when it is very hot, she says she wants to rest. But she only pretends to rest. Really she wants to make her clothes. She does quite good work.

I am a child, I cannot make my clothes properly. I still have to practise. My mother tells me that when I am bigger, I will have to make them myself. Women have to make clothes, they have to do everything themselves. They have to embroider their clothes. Even if you are no good at it, you still have to do it.

I have to learn. My mother teaches me. Every girl has to learn how to do it. Me and my friends play at making clothes. When I am in the right mood, I can do many different styles. I am much better at making clothes than my sister.

DAY SCHOOL IN THE FIELDS - Meesia

Meesia is 15 years old and is the elder sister of Amiyo (see Akha Girl). She works in the fields every day but also attends the village school early in the mornings and late at night. During the day, the village school, which is part of a Thai-Canada development project, goes to the fields to carry on the teaching.

MEESIA: There are twenty pupils and three teachers at my school. They are very nice, they are good teachers. They are kind to the children. We go to the school early in the mornings before we go to the fields.

Every day we have to go to work in the fields. During the day, they come to the fields to teach. We make it very difficult for the teachers. But we have to help our parents work in the fields. I feel sorry for the teachers. Sometimes we have to work in different fields. Sometimes the pupils are all spread out in different fields. The teachers have to walk quite far to teach us. If we work close to each other, it is much easier for them.

At my school we have one woman teacher. She is fat. Every day she has to walk to the fields to teach us. She often looks very tired. Sometimes it is very hot, especially on the way back to the village in the afternoons. She's always hungry. The other two teachers are men. They have no problems. One of them is Lisu or Lahu. They are strong, they don't mind walking to the fields.

In the evening, we go to school from seven o'clock to nine o'clock. We have a big lamp at school, it's very bright.

NEW YEAR - Laoair

Laoair's (see Spirit Gate - Meeting - Ground - Opium, Prison, and the Seven Japanese) favourite time of year, along with most Akha people, is New Year. It is during the two New Year celebrations that Laoair and his wife can relax and enjoy themselves, temporarily oblivious to the hardships of their lives.

INTERVIEWER: When is Akha New Year? Is it the same as the Swing Festival?

LAOAIR: We have Akha New Year twice a year. The first one is for the men, and the second one for the women. We have the men's New Year after every family has finished the rice harvest. The festival is for our ancestors. We believe the ancestors are good spirits who help us to have good crops and enough food, and to be happy.

The festival is held in December every year. The spirit-man decides the exact date. It lasts for four days. The first day is for praying to the spirits who give everything to the Akha people. We pound sticky rice and vegetables, and salt, and offer it to the spirits. Some we keep to eat.

On the second day we sacrifice a pig for the spirits. Later we can eat it. Friends who visit the family can also share the pork. The second day is the important day. Nobody can go out of the village. It is also the day for the men to wear nice clothes. Every man has fun. Most men play top-spinning.

The third day is as important as the second. We drink whisky, play with the spinning tops and generally celebrate the New Year.

The fourth day is not so important. Anyone can go anywhere they like, but they cannot work, and they cannot sacrifice anything. This is the last day of the men's New Year.

After New Year, the men start clearing the land to prepare the rice fields for the coming year. At this time of year we think a lot about nature, and hope everything is going to be all right.

INTERVIEWER: What about the New Year for the women? How does it start?

LAOAIR: Women's New Year is the Swing Festival, it is the special time for the women. It is usually held near the end of August. Before the festival, about one or two months before, the women have to go into town to buy special things for their clothes. They have to get the material to make their shirts and skirts, their leggings, and their head-dresses, for themselves and for their children, to wear on the festival days. The men buy their own things.

One week before the festival, Akha people prepare food and firewood for the four days of the festival. Nobody can go out of the village during the festival.

The first day is the same as with the men's festival, and the second day is similar, except we kill chickens and not pigs. The third day is the day when the spirit-man starts the Swing Festival, and each family sacrifices another chicken. The spirit-man asks the mother-earth spirit and the ancestor spirits to help with the festival.

Everyone has to work together to make the swing. Some look for vines to make the ropes, some dig the holes for the posts, and some cut the bamboo for the frame. When the work is finished, the spirit-man is the first person to use the swing. After the spirit-man, all the women and girls use the swing until the end of the day.

On the fourth day, the last day, the spirit-man is the last person to use the swing. Then the Swing Festival is over.

During the women's New Year, all the women wear their best clothes. Whatever they have that is beautiful, they wear during the festival days. In Akha life, nothing is as special as the New Years. When we have the New Year festivals, everybody forgets about the work in the fields, and about being tired. For four days twice a year, we forget.

CHAPTER THREE
LAHU

1) **Refugees** - Jou, 43.
   Why Jou and her family left Laos, and the story of her two daughters now living in America.
2) **From Spirits to Christianity** - Jou, 43.
   Why Jou converted to Christianity despite her belief in spirits.
3) **When the Sky and the Earth Come Together** - Nagah, 17.
   Nagah tells of her first, unsuccessful marriage to a Lahu man, and of her second, recent happy marriage to a Thai.
4) **Married at Twelve to a Bad Old Man** - Nasee, 15.
   Nasee speaks openly of her bad experiences with her former husband.
5) **Selling Children** - Boon, 26.
   Boon relates the tragic story of how her husband sold their two children in order to buy opium.
6) **Bird Catching** - Ben Na-Kiu, 26.
   Ben talks about trapping birds and hunting.
7) **Going to Town** - Mou, 15.
   Mou's impressions and fears on going to a Thai town.

REFUGEES - Jou

Jou is about 43 years old, and lives with her second husband and two of the five children from her previous marriage in the Lahu enclave in the Hmong village of Kiew Khan. She is a refugee from Laos. Her house is a small simple two-room bamboo hut raised on stilts.

INTERVIEWER: How long ago did you leave Laos?

JOU: I left when Laos became communist, that was about fourteen years ago now. When I first came to Thailand, I lived in Ban Dong refugee camp. I stayed there for about three years. The camp has now been shut. Later I moved to Huai Look village, then after two or three years, I came to Kiew Khan.

My first husband died in Ban Huai Look when the youngest child was two years old. Now the child is nine or ten. I have three girls and two boys. My two eldest daughters married Hmong men. Both of them got married when they were at Chiangkham refugee camp. Now they are both living in America with their Hmong husbands. Before they went there, they had to learn English. Now they are happy in America.

I think there's no chance for me to see my daughters again. Sometimes I think my daughters will come to visit me in the village, but really I know they've only a little money and can't come to see me. I think it's impossible.

It was easy for them to go to America, even though they had no money, because the American government paid for them. Before, when they lived in the refugee camp, they got everything free, the American government paid for everything. They had a good life in the camp. But they had no freedom, no independence. They couldn't just go anywhere they wanted. When they wanted to go somewhere, they first had to report to the camp officials and ask permission. It was always too much trouble.

I left the refugee camp a long time ago, but my daughters stayed in the camp until they got married. Now one daughter has four children. I've never seen their children or their husbands.

INTERVIEWER: What did your daughters and sons-in-law do in the refugee camp?

JOU: One son-in-law was a teacher of Hmong in the camp, the other one didn't have a job, although he had studied in the past. Both of them could speak English. In the refugee camp, if anybody wanted to live in America, they had to speak good English. They had to learn English, and practise it, and be clever. It wasn't always easy to go to America.

INTERVIEWER: And what about you, have you married again?

JOU: Yes, my new husband is quite young, younger than me. He doesn't do much. He spends most of his time smoking opium, although sometimes he does go hunting. He is much younger than me. He doesn't want to help me in the fields. He has no children, but I have a son and a daughter living with me, so it's difficult for me to ask him to help. I have to work very hard. He only comes to help me when he feels like it. We're poor.

Before, when we were in Laos, we were quite rich. Every family had cows and buffaloes and chickens. If we were short of money, we could sell some animals. We could do what we wanted, Laos was our country. But when we left Laos, we couldn't carry much. It was difficult to bring things to Thailand. We couldn't bring the animals. We had only our clothes and some silver coins to carry with us. So, now we are poor.

In Laos, rich people had machines. They couldn't bring their machines to Thailand when they fled. We had lots of rice, lands, and farms. We left everything in Laos and fled because we thought we might be killed if we stayed. We thought it was better to get away from the country.

In Laos we had plenty of rice to eat, and plenty in reserve. Everything was easy for us. We had a good life in Laos, much better than the lives we have now, here in Thailand.

FROM SPIRITS TO CHRISTIANITY - Jou

> *Jou (see Refugees) was converted to Christianity when she was living in Laos. She admits that she doesn't really know much about Christianity and is not a devout Christian. Jou has a good relationship with all the other Lahu people in the village, as well as with many of the Hmong living nearby. She can speak Hmong, Lao and Thai, in addition to her native Lahu Shi.*

INTERVIEWER: Do many people in the village believe in spirits?

JOU: Not many. Most people became Christians a long time ago. Me and my family became Christians when we were living in Laos, about thirty years ago. In Laos we had a Father who taught us about being Christian. He was a Laotian, not a farang. More than thirty years ago, a long time ago when my parents were still alive, we believed in spirits. We sacrificed chickens and pigs to the spirits.

Sometimes if somebody was ill, we sacrificed a chicken to the spirits. Then the spirits could say why the person was ill. Sometimes a bad spirit would make a person ill. Then we had to get a good spirit to help, because a good spirit, for example the house spirit, is more powerful than a bad one. Or sometimes there were bad spirits in the forest, spirits with no relatives. If people die in the jungle, or if they die in a car or bus crash, or if animals kill them, and nobody knows they are dead, then there is nobody to make the offerings of food to their spirits. It is these spirits that make people ill, because they want to eat chicken or pork. If we sacrifice chickens or pigs to the bad spirits, the people get better.

INTERVIEWER: How do you know that the bad spirits accept your offerings?

JOU: We have belived in spirits for a long time. After offering the chicken or the pig, the sick person gets better, usually after one or two days.

INTERVIEWER: Why did you change your mind and become a Christian?

JOU: Er, we had sacrificed chickens to the spirits for a long time, we got lazy. We thought it was too much trouble to make offerings of food to the spirits. Sometimes we had no chickens or pigs for the spirits, and no money to buy more. Sometimes somebody was ill for a long time, for months and months. We had to make offerings for a long time, but still the person was ill. We decided it was better to take them to hospital. Some of them died, but some even now are still alive.

The Father gave us medicines and taught us how to use them. He was a very nice person. He didn't want anything in return. He taught us that when we were ill, very ill, if we waited for too long before going to hospital, we could die.

Sometimes we sacrificed to the spirits when somebody was ill, but we were never sure that they would get better. The best way was to take them to the hospital.

Some people listened to the Father, and some did not. He wasn't angry if anybody ignored him. He had a good heart. Sometimes he gave clothes to us.

In Laos we had a good life. It made me think about Christianity. Everybody we knew, all our friends, were Christians. We had many Christian friends. So we changed our beliefs and became Christian. We are still Christian.

WHEN THE SKY AND THE EARTH COME TOGETHER - Nagah

Nagah is 17 years old and is married to a Thai man from a nearby Thai village. He is her second husband. Her first husband was a Lahu man from a village in Fang District, Chiang Mai. On both occasions she was practically sold to her husbands by her parents who are both opium addicts. She now lives in her husband's village and is generally happy with her husband and her life. She and her husband often visit her parents and friends in the village.

NAGAH: Now I am living in a Thai village with a Thai husband. I used to live in Fang, in Chiang Mai Province. My first husband was from Fang District. Living in Fang was good. We had a good life. The Lahu there built houses like Thai houses. My husband worked for Thais. Sometimes I worked for Thais as well, but usually it was only my husband who worked.

INTERVIEWER: Why did you get divorced from your husband?

NAGAH: He was no good. Every night he went to visit other women. I had to sleep alone every night. I told him to stay at home sometimes. I was frightened to sleep alone because my house was near to the Thai people's houses. I knew it was dangerous to sleep alone at night. When I told him to stop visiting other women, he got angry. We always had big arguments. He used to hit me. I was very sad. He was a bad husband. I was unlucky, especially because my parents lived a long way away.

INTERVIEWER: Was your husband a good man before you were married?

NAGAH: I don't know whether he was good or bad before we got married, I only knew him a short time. After we got married, we went straight to Fang. The first two years of being married were not too bad. But after that he started to be bad. He married me, so he should have been honest, so why did he have to go and visit women every night? I didn't do anything wrong. He told me he wanted to leave me. I had to think about it a lot. Then I agreed, and we separated. I had to leave the house.

I went back to live with my parents. My husband didn't take me, I had to go on my own. I took the bus from Fang. I was a bit frightened on the bus, I was afraid I might get lost. But it wasn't too difficult, I had learned to read some Thai before I left. When I didn't know where I was, I just asked a policeman.

I'd lived in Fang for three years. After living in Fang, I lived with my parents. I helped them in the fields. Sometimes I worked for the Hmong people. I did any sort of work. It was very difficult to make money.

INTERVIEWER: Did you have children?

NAGANH: No, I had no children. I was on the pill for three years. If I'd had children, it'd have been very difficult to divorce, I'd have had nothing for my children.

Even me, I had to come back to live with my parents. I'm a woman, it's difficult to do anything, difficult to make money.

INTERVIEWER: Do you still live with your parents?

NAGAH: No, I don't live with my parents now, I live in a Thai village. I've been married for two months already. My new husband is Thai. He's older than me, but he's a nice man.

INTERVIEWER: How did you meet him?

NAGAH: He came to my village and a friend of my parents recognised him and introduced us. Then he came to my house. He often came to smoke with my parents. After that, he got to know me. He asked me to marry him. He asked me just like that, out of the blue. I told him I didn't want to marry him. I didn't like him, he's a lot older than me. He's thirty-eight and I am seventeen. He's been married three times before to Thai women. So I said no.

I didn't like him smoking with my parents. He smoked with my parents every day. I'm fed up with people smoking opium. He bought opium for my parents to smoke. They liked him because of the opium he bought for them. They offered me to him.

He paid six hundred baht to my parents and came to live with me at my house for a while. Then he took me to his village. At first I missed my house, my sister and my village. But it wasn't too hard living with Thais, I'd lived with Thais before.

INTERVIEWER: Is your husband good to you?

NAGAH: Yes, of course, he's a good man, a nice man. He loves me and gives me all his money. When he wants some money, he asks me, and I give him some. But I don't like it that he's older than me. Sometimes I try and tell him that we must get divorced because my friends in the village talk about him and me. They say he's not my husband, but my father. It's embarrassing. Every time when I mention divorce, he tells me he will kill me and cut off my head. I never know whether he is joking or not.

INTERVIEWER: You are lucky if your husband is a nice man, a good man, if he gives you all the money he has.

NAGAH: Oh, I agree, especially when compared to my first husband. My first husband once made seven hundred baht in one day, and spent all of it on women in one day.

My Thai husband smokes opium, but he can earn money himself. He never spends money on women or whisky. He stays with me all day, and then when it gets dark he sleeps with me the whole night. Every day.

He's not a rich man, but I am happy to live with him. He doesn't hit me. For me that's important. He loves me a lot. If he didn't love me, I couldn't live with him.

I've seen Thai men. Most of them, if they love their wives, then they love them a lot, they really love them. But if they don't love their wives, then they're very bad men, sometimes hitting their wives, sometimes kicking them. They're always in a bad mood. I saw many Thais when I lived in the village in Fang.

Thai and Lahu men are very different. A Thai man is great in bed. My Thai husband is very different from my previous Lahu husband. My Thai husband can make love all night, especially after smoking a little bit of opium. And he's very good at kissing, kissing everywhere.

NEIGHBOUR: No, no, not true, not true at all. Sure, after smoking a lot of opium, Lahu men are not interested in sex, but if they've been smoking for just a little while, then of course they like it, they like it a lot, they can make love for the whole night. But if they smoke every day, then after many years the penis dies. Thais must be the same as Lahus.

INTERVIEWER: Nagah, do you have a Thai name?

NAGAH: Yes, I have a Thai name. My husband took me to live with him in the Thai village. His neighbours didn't like my name. 'Nagah' is a bad name for Thai people. It is the name of a bird in a Thai story. In the story the bird stays at home during the day but as soon as it starts to get dark the bird goes out. Thais think the bird is a spirit bird, so they gave me another name. My new name is Suphan. That's my Thai name.

When I first went to the village, I was very shy. I was the only Lahu person living there. I told my husband it would be better to live in my parent's house and asked him to take me home. He told me he'd take me home the next day. The following day I told him I must go that day. But he said the next day again, and again.

Every day he said the same. But now I don't mind living there, now I am happy.

Really Lahu people don't like divorce, they like to keep one husband, one wife. Getting married is like when the sky and the earth come together. Lahu people believe in spirits, and in the world there is one big sky spirit and one big earth spirit.

MARRIED AT TWELVE TO A BAD OLD MAN - Nasee

Nasee is 15 years old and is the younger sister of Nagah (see When The Sky And The Earth Come Together). When she was twelve years old she was married/sold to a Lahu man from a nearby Lahu village. The man paid her parents sixty baht. Nasee managed to divorce him after two years of unhappy marriage by paying him three hundred baht. She now has a boyfriend from her village whom she hopes to marry soon. She lives with her parents and works in the family's fields and also in fields belonging to her Hmong neighbours.

INTERVIEWER: How are you Nasee?

NAWEE: Oh, not very well. It's raining and it's difficult to go to the fields. And it's cold, very cold.

INTERVIEWER: Is your husband at home today?

NASEE: I haven't got a husband now. We separated eight months ago. I didn't like him any more. He was older than me. He was a bad man.

INTERVIEWER: Why did you marry him in the first place then?

NASEE: I knew before that he was a bad man. I think I never loved him. I really didn't like him before, but he liked me a lot. He was older than me, he wanted to marry a young girl like me. He bought opium for my parents. Then he asked them if he could marry me.

My parents asked me to marry him, but I said no. A little bit later, I had to go to the fields for a few days. When I was away, my parents offered me to him. Then he came to the fields to see me. We slept together in the fields. Later he took me back to stay in my parent's house for a while.

INTERVIEWER: Where did your husband come from?

NASEE: He was Lahu, from Huai Tu village. Sometimes he took me to stay in his house in Huai Tu, but usually we stayed in my parent's field house.

INTERVIEWER: Why did you leave him? Did you have a big argument?

NASEE: (She is silent)

INTERVIEWER: Maybe you had a problem. Please tell me. But if you don't want to, then never mind.

NASEE: I left him because it was very difficult to live with him. He was a bad old man. I couldn't live with him anymore. Sometimes he beat me. My parents never used to hit me when I lived at home. But he did. When I lived with him I couldn't get away from him to play, I couldn't get away for a bit of fun. And...and er, when he wanted to sleep with me, really I didn't like it.

When he made love to me, it hurt a lot. He was quite big. Once I didn't let him, and he got very angry and hit me. Then I left him and went to my parent's house. A few days later he followed me and said he was sorry. He was friendly to me again. He bought some opium for my father. My father told me to go back and live with him. So I went to live with him again.

But I found it very difficult to live with him. I didn't love him. How could I have fun? How could I be happy with him? I didn't let him make love to me, so he kicked me to the ground. I hurt my bottom and my back. I couldn't walk for a few days. Later, when I got better, I left him again. Of course I don't ever want to go back to him. It has already been eight months since I left him.

INTERVIEWER: Are you happy now that you live alone and have no husband?

NASEE: I'm happy to be living with my parents. My parents are very good to me.

NEIGHBOUR: Ah, now she has a new boyfriend, maybe soon they will get married. They are at it every day now.

NASEE: No we don't, we don't do it every day. (She laughs). That's crazy.

INTERVIEWER: Nasee, how different are the two men? Do you mind talking openly?

NASEE: Every girl, when she grows up, has to make love. Everybody. Now sitting here we are only girls and women, we don't need to be shy. When I was married, I was frightened of my husband. I was very frightened of him. I didn't like it when the sun went down because that meant it was getting dark and I had to let him make love to me. It always hurt so much. When we made love, he would at first try and be careful, but it still always hurt a lot. Then he would get cross and be rougher.

When my boyfriend makes love to me it never hurts, it's nice, I always have a nice feeling. I like him. I like him to make love to me. My boyfriend is from the village. At night he comes to sleep in my house after my parents have already gone to bed. We've been sleeping together for over one month now. My parents know, but they don't mind. They've never seen us actually doing it.

INTERVIEWER: Are you on the pill? You know, you have to be careful, you could easily get pregnant.

NASEE: I'm not worried about getting pregnant. It's good to be pregnant. I don't want to take the pill. My elder sister told me that if you go on the pill, you lose weight and get ugly. We make love together so we don't mind if we have a baby. If a girl and boy make love and have fun, then they should have something special, something different and and maybe face difficulties together.

INTERVIEWER: How old are you Nasee? How old was your first husband?

NASEE: I am fifteen and my ex-husband is thirty. He was fifteen years older than me. He's had a lot of bad experiences with sex. He'd been married twice before and both women left him because they didn't like to have sex with him. They thought it was better to leave him.

My new boyfriend makes love to me often and it never hurts, it's good fun. When girls are fifteen they can make love every day, but twelve year old girls cannot, if they do, they might hurt themselves.

INTERVIEWER: You only have one big room in your house, one room for the whole family, it must be difficult to have any privacy. How do you manage?

NASEE: In my house we have one big room for everybody, for sitting, for sleeping, eating and smoking. Everybody has to sleep together. Before we go to bed, we go out somewhere, anywhere where there are no people, so we can make love. Sometimes we do it behind the house. My elder sister and my brother-in-law do the same. But during the rainy season we cannot do it outside, it's too muddy, too difficult. We can't go outside, so we have to make love in the house when everybody has fallen asleep.

When I was young, I saw my parents doing it. They didn't know I saw. In the morning me and my sister joked about them making love the night before. My parents knew we were joking about them, so they hit me and my sister so that we wouldn't talk about them again.

Sometimes my sister and my brother-in-law make love in the house. My brother-in-law is Thai. He likes to kiss my sister a lot. He makes love to my sister for a long time. My sister likes him a lot. She told me her husband is a good husband with a good heart. She said he likes to give her pleasure. He does it with my sister every day. And he likes to kiss her for a long time.

My parents are happy to see my sister and my brother-in-law in love together.

SELLING CHILDREN - Boon Seblang

Boon is 26 years old and lives alone with her youngest child. In the past her husband sold two of their children to help pay for his opium addiction - an addiction which later killed him. Boon works in her fields to support herself and her child, but also accepts help from neighbours in return for sexual favours. She says she has no intention of ever marrying again.

INTERVIEWER: How many children have you had?

BOON: I've had six children altogether, three of them were stillborn. Of the three that lived, I've only got one at home because my husband sold two of them - a son and a daughter. The girl was sold to some Hmong people at Kiew Nam Kham village, and the boy was sold to a Hmong family here at Kiew Khan. Now my daughter at Kiew Nam Kham has already died.

INTERVIEWER: How did she die?

BOON: She died of malaria. If she'd lived, she'd have been ten years old now. She was sold for Bht. 3,300. She was a little bit expensive because the buyers could use her to work for them and then later marry her off. The buyer'd have made a lot of money, because the man who'd have married her'd have had to pay a lot in silver coins for her. In Thai money it'd have been about Bht. 33,000. In a Hmong family, when the daughter gets married, it's really the same as being sold.

My son was a little bit cheaper - Bht. 3,000. The man who bought my son lives in the village. He was sold when he was two years old. Now he is nine.

INTERVIEWER: Were you sad when your children were sold?

BOON: I was very sad. In my heart I didn't want to sell them. I carried them for nine months when I was pregnant with them. I had a lot of pain when I gave birth. They were my flesh and blood.

Lahu women have no influence over their husbands, the men have to be dominant, the men have to be the boss. The women can't be strong. I couldn't complain to my husband when he sold my children because I'm a Lahu woman, even though I was very sad, even though he was selling my children, selling my heart, selling everything I had.

I still remember the day. That day I went to work in the fields for the morning. I came back from the fields to have lunch and couldn't see my son. I asked my husband where my son was. I thought maybe someone was looking after him. My husband seemed a bit strange. He said someone was looking after the boy and that I was not to worry. He looked sad when he said that. He didn't want to talk anymore. I thought he was in a funny mood because he needed some opium. Usually when he had no opium, he was in bad mood and didn't want to talk. But really he was in a strange mood because he'd sold my son.

INTERVIEWER: Why did he sell your children?

BOON: He sold them because he needed money for opium. I didn't want to sell them, but I couldn't say anything. If I'd complained, or said something, he'd have hit me. Even if I'd cried, he'd have hit me. I couldn't do anything.

My daughter was sold when she was six months old. My son was two years old when he was sold. Now my son lives with a family near here. I still feel very attached to him, but he's not interested in me or my little baby. Sometimes he comes to play near my house. He looks just like the other children. He looks Lahu, not Hmong. He doesn't call me mother, or mum.

I feel guilty about my son. It's difficult to say anything to him. I can't tell him I love him very much, or that I want him very much. I think he still remembers I'm his mum, because he's never friendly to me.

Now my husband has died. He smoked too much opium, and died. He died young.

BIRD CATCHING - Ben Na-kiu

Ben is about 25 years old and is married with one child. When not helping his wife in the fields, Ben spends much of his time out in the forest hunting birds - usually green parrots and minah birds.

INTERVIEWER: How many birds did you get today? Can you explain how you catch them?

BEN: Early in the morning, I set the cage and put some bait inside. I usually use fruit or rice. Then I leave the cage up a tree in the jungle. But before I leave the cage, I have to put a bird inside. The captive bird makes a noise, and the wild birds hear the noise and go inside. And then the trap shuts.

Sometimes it's a male bird inside the cage who sings to attract a female, sometimes it's a female inside the cage who sings to attract a male.

INTERVIEWER: When is a good time to catch birds?

BEN: Any time when there's no rain is a good time. The morning is a good time because the birds are out looking for food. The best time is early in the morning and late in the afternoon.

INTERVIEWER: How many birds have you caught from your very first day hunting until now?

BEN: Oh, one hundred , two hundred, male and female, small birds and big birds, baby birds and very old birds.

Oh, it's difficult to remember all of them. I didn't count them.

Lahu people are very good at hunting. Me, I got five birds in three days. We catch them to sell, but we eat them if nobody wants to buy them. Thai people often come to the village to buy birds so I don't need to go to the town with them. I sell one bird for fifty baht, sometimes forty baht if it's difficult to sell. Some people are very mean. They don't want to pay forty baht, they want to pay only thirty baht.

INTERVIEWER: Do you only look for birds when you go hunting, or do you also look for pigs and deer?

BEN: In the past I used to only look for wild boar. But now it's difficult. It's very difficult to find boar, because there're too many hunters. If I wanted to hunt pigs, I'd have to go at night. Once, there were many boar, I used to get one every day. There was even too much to eat. In those days, my wife had to dry the meat so we could keep it for later.

INTERVIEWER: Do you have to do anything for the spirits before you go hunting?

BEN: Oh, that's not important. Hunting is nothing to do with spirits. Two things are important, good dogs, clever dogs, and good guns. The dog is very important. Every time you go hunting for deer or boar, you need a very clever dog.

Sometimes we go to Huai Tu and Huai Sa villages to hunt. And often we go to Doi Luang. Many animals come from Laos. They cross the river near Huai Tu, and then go to Doi Luang mountain. There's a lot of fruit for the animals to eat at Doi Luang. It has a lot of thick jungle, so it's a good place for the animals to stay during the cold season.

Now there aren't many animals. There're too many hunters. Everybody shoots and makes a noise. They make the animals run further away. Once, if you heard a gun, you would think somebody'd got a deer or wild boar, but now, now you can hear a gun go off every day. Sometimes even the children shoot.

GOING TO TOWN - Mou

Mou is 15 years old and has been married since she was ten. She calls her husband "father" and spends most of the day playing with the children in the village. Her husband works in the fields to support them both.

INTERVIEWER: Have you ever been to a Thai town?

MOU: Yes, I've been twice to Chiangkhong town. Once with my mother for shopping just before New Year, and once with my husband in the Hmong car when we didn't have to pay.

INTERVIEWER: How different is the town from your village?

MOU: I went to the town, I had fun. Many things are different from my Lahu village. The Thai people in the town are very pretty, and they're nice people. They have nice clothes and have pretty things in their hair, expensive things.

It's very busy in the town, there're many people. A lot of things are being sold. The Thais have very nice clothes, very expensive clothes. And there're many cars in the town. I'm frightened of the cars, and I'm frightened of the people. They look at me in such a terrible way.

We live in the mountains and there aren't any cars, except in the Hmong village where they have a pick-up truck. If we want to go somewhere, we have to go in the Hmong car.

INTERVIEWER: Would you ever want to live in a Thai town?

MOU: No. I couldn't live with the Thai people in the town. Thais look strange, it's difficult to talk to them, and I'm frightened of getting run over. And I'm frightened of getting lost. But riding in the car to the town is good fun, especially when the road is bumpy.

CHAPTER FOUR
HMONG

1) **New Village** - Laojan, 23.
   Laojan explains why his parents left Laos and how the family came to be living in Kiew Khan.

2) **Laogwa - Old Headman** - Laogwa, 42.
   Two episodes from Laogwa's life - the burning down of the hospital in which he worked, and his appointment as headman of Kiew Khan.

3) **Grandfather-General** - Laoleuer, 42.
   Laoleuer tells of his grandfather and the fall of Laos in 1974/75 and compares free and comfortable Siam with you-cannot-be-lazy communist Laos.

4) **Condoms** - Somchai, 26.
   Somchai, the government appointed village health worker, describes with humour the problems and difficulties he had in trying to introduce birth control into the village.

5) **Finding a Bride** - Somchai, 26.
   Somchai outlines the Hmong marriage customs past and present.

6) **First Love** - Namai, 23.
   Namai relates how she was ordered by her boyfriend's father to turn away her first real love.

7) **Married to a Thai Boy** - Nayua, 15.
   Nayua tells of her new life married to a Thai man and living "down" the mountain.

8) **Staying Single** - Nadoa, 20.
   Nadoa has looked about her and decided marriage is not for her. She explains why.

9) **Moving in with the In-Laws** - Nalee, 21.
Nalee from Ban Giang village explains why she is working for the family in Kiew Khan and not for her family in Ban Giang.

10) **Little Girl** - Namai, 4.
Namai explains why she now likes to wear clothes and tells of the games she and her friend Bor like to play.

11) **School Leaver** - Nabai, 11.
Nabai talks about her school and why she had to leave.

12) **Hunting** - Laojongser, 42.
Everything you could want to know about hunting wild boar from the most experienced hunter in Kiew Khan.

13) **The Spirits of the Boar and Gun** - Laojongser, 42.
The how and why of the hunters' spirit rituals.

14) **Hunting Accident** - Laojongser, 42.
Details of an accidental shooting in a maize field.

15) **My Husband** - Three Telling Stories - Najor, 41.
Najor gives three episodes from her husband's life to illustrate her misfortune in marrying such a man.

16) **The First Farang** - Somchai, 26.
Somchai describes his early impressions of farang who came to his village.

17) **Old Woman** - Maethao, 86.
An old woman on the subject of farang.

NEW VILLAGE - Laojan

Laojan is 23, married, and spends much of his time hunting in the hills surrounding Kiew Khan village. He is one of the regular takraw players to be found every day playing outside the village school just before sundown.

LAOJAN: Doi Luang mountain was the first place Hmong people came to from Laos, about sixty to sixty-five years ago. My mother and father came from Laos. My father, along with many other people, heard about Doi Luang Prae Muang and liked the idea of going there to live. They didn't know anything else about Thailand.

My father heard that a friend of his lived at Doi Luang. He went to see his friend's family. They told him that Doi Luang was a high mountain with a lot of jungle and just one small village and that it would be good to go there. My father told my mother they had to go to Thailand. This is the Hmong way.

Because we have to move the village whenever the water dries up or when there are not enough trees, we built the village near a waterfall and close to thick jungle. At Doi Luang we had plenty of water, plenty for drinking and for washing. It was a good place to live.

It is the Hmong way of life that if we move somewhere, we have to cut down many trees to build our homes. If we cut too many, there're not enough left and the area becomes very dry. Then there's no water. Water and wood are so important in our lives. Kiew Khan is our last village, here we must end our lives. There is no place to move on to any more.

Hmong people marry, they have children, and their children have children. So there're many people and the villages get too big. My parents were still young when they lived at Doi Luang. I was their first child. We left Doi Luang and moved to Kiew Khan about twenty years ago.

When we first came to Kiew Khan, there were only seven families. There was jungle all around the village. My father has told me that there were tigers in the jungle in those days. When the men went out to cut down the bamboo to clear the land for the rice fields, and had to stay the night outside, they built field-houses four metres off the ground, really, four metres off the ground. They wanted to keep well away from the animals. In the past, people were frightened of the animals, but now they're frightened of us.

LAOGWA - THE OLD HEADMAN - Laogwa

Laogwa was born in Laos in the late 1940s. During the 1950s his family moved to Thailand to live in Huai Haan village at Doi Luang Prae Muang. In the mid 1960s, Laogwa, along with two of his friends, was singled out by an American aid official to be trained as a medical orderly in Chiang Mai. He was fifteen years old. After training, he returned to Huai Haan to work in the village hospital.

LAOGWA: One day a Thai man came to me. He pretended to be a distant cousin. He asked me to go with him to see his friend who was very ill and couldn't walk to the hospital. I went to see him at his house. He wasn't so bad. He could walk very well. After having given him an injection, I began to pack everything away. I wanted to return to the hospital. But the man who was pretending to be my cousin had a gun. He didn't want me to return to the hospital. I told him I had to go back to the hospital that day. But they wouldn't let me go.

That night they killed my friends who worked at the hospital. I was very frightened. For sure they would kill me if I went back to work at the hospital. Some people were communists in the village, but nobody knew who. I decided to leave the village. I worried about my things which were still in my room at the hospital, including my papers, but really I had nothing special so I left them. Later they burned down the hospital and killed some more people who worked there. I was very frightened then, so I went to stay in Laos for nearly a year.

INTERVIEWER: Why didn't they kill you?

LAOGWA: Because I worked for the government and for the Americans. It was more serious to kill me.

INTERVIEWER: Why did they burn the hospital?

LAOGWA: They were jealous of what the Thai government was doing. They wanted only the communists to help the people.

Laogwa stayed in Laos for one year, living with a cousin on a farm. In 1967 he returned to Thailand and went back to Chiangmai for further training. For nearly a year he worked for the Thai police as a translator in order to help improve contact between the police and the Hmong people of Chiang Mai and Chiang Rai provinces. His wife didn't like him working for the government, and also didn't like Chiang Mai, and so in 1970 they left Chiang Mai and went to Kiew Khan. His family was the first family from Doi Luang to move to Kiew Khan. At about the same time, an old friend also moved to Kiew Khan from Doi Luang. This old friend, Laoda, was chosen to be headman.

LAOGWA: Laoda was tired of being the headman. He had to work for his family and for the people in the village. He had many things to do for his family. He had to look after the rice fields, the cows and the buffaloes. He had many children. He had many problems being the headman.

In 1983 Laoda called the people to a meeting. He asked the people what they thought about me. He told them he wanted to stop being the headman. He told them to choose me to become the new headman.

The people thought I was quite clever, and they knew I liked to help the people in the village. And the people agreed that I was the right age and could read and write Thai. Also they knew I knew many places because I had lived in Chiang Mai. They also knew I had enough money to pay for the fare if ever I had to go somewhere on village business.

It was difficult for me to say no. I understood that there were many problems with being a good headman. If the people didn't want me to be the headman, it didn't matter to me. I didn't mind. But the people chose me, so I became the headman.

I helped the village have a good relationship with the authorities, and I helped them build the water system, and I taught them how to build a toilet. Building the toilet was the government's idea, not mine.

I was the headman for five years. After five years, I wanted to stop being the headman. There were too many problems with the people in the village. And also, somebody with an education wanted to be the headman. But that's good for me. Now I have more time for my family. Now I can help my wife and children with their work.

GRANDFATHER-GENERAL - Laoleuer

Laoleuer is 42 years old and married with seven children, the eldest being twenty and the youngest just fourteen months. He is a member of the Border Patrol Police and is stationed in the village.

LAOLEUER: My great-grandparents lived in China. When there was fighting in China, they left and went to Laos. They lived in the area bordered by China, Burma and Thailand. They died in Laos.

In the past, Laos was a colony of France. The French administered Laos. The whole border area and the whole of the Mekong river was really a part of Laos. The French changed the border. Now the Mekong is the border.

My grandparents came to Thailand. They had my father in Thailand. My father lived in many places. He lived in Huai Haan. He married in Huai Haan and went to live in Doi Luang village. I was born in Doi Luang. I have been living in Kiew Khan village for twenty-one years.

My grandparents had family in Laos. They didn't want to come to Thailand because they were aristocracy. They were generals in Laos. They tried to stop the Vietnamese communists. Originally the generals in Laos were not Laotian, but Hmong, they had a Hmong background.

My grandfather was a general. Some people who worked for the President of Laos were worried about the serious fighting. Some of them went over to the communists. They put their names on a piece of paper. Many people signed. Only my grandfather did not want to sign. Only him. They asked him to see the names of the people who had signed. So my grandfather decided to come to Thailand.

It was difficult to come to the border. If he went by plane or helicopter, it would be easy for the communists to follow him. The communists had planes and helicopters. My grandfather could not fly from the centre of Laos to Thailand because the Red Lao, the Laotian comunists, they knew who my grandfather was.

My grandfather had to tell one of his men to tell the people who worked for him in Bangkok to get a plane or helicopter to wait for him on the Thai border. He went by jeep from the centre of Laos to the Thai border. He had many soldiers. They followed him to Bangkok at the same time that Laos fell to the communists.

Many people cried when Laos fell. They were waiting for my grandfather to help them. But the communists were eager to catch my grandfather because he was an important man.

During the last five days, my grandfather's soldiers came to Thailand by jeep and aeroplane. They waited with flags to see my grandfather in Thailand. They stayed in Thailand for nearly one month, then they left the country. Many went to America.

INTERVIEWER : When did Laos fall?

LAOLEUER: I'm not sure, maybe fifteen years ago. Some of the soldiers died, some went to the jungles, and some came to Thailand. They had no general to look after them. It was a good time for the Vietnamese communists to go to Laos. Even now Laos is a colony of Communist Vietnam.

Many people don't like the communist laws. Some people like them, some don't. Even if you don't like it, there is nothing you can do about the Vietnamese communists. You can't refuse if they tell you to do something, you must do everything they tell you.

Laos is very different from Siam. Siam is very comfortable. If you want to do anything, you can do it. In Laos you can't be lazy. Even if you have a cow or chickens or a pig, you cannot eat them, you have to look after them for the government. If you want to kill them to eat, you must first report this to the government. You must report it at least a week before you want to kill them. You have to explain why you want to do it. You can say your wife is ill or your mother is very old and would like to eat meat, or you can say you want to have a celebration for the family, or maybe you can say you want to kill the animals to make an offering to the spirits. If the government says no, if they do not give you permission, then you cannot eat any meat, you can't kill the animals.

If you kill and eat the animals without telling the government, the government will punish you. They will think you killed the animals because you wanted to leave Laos and go to Thailand.

INTERVIEWER: Where did you live when your grandfather was living in Laos?

LAOLEUER: Oh, I have lived in Thailand for a long time.

Sometimes my grandfather came to Thailand. But I never saw him. I am too dirty, too poor, it was not important for me to see him. If I had wanted to see him, I would have had to sign my name in a book and explain to his men why I wanted to see him. But my parents have seen him in Thailand. And my uncle has been to see him in Bangkok sometimes.

INTERVIEWER: Is your grandfather still alive? Where does he live now?

LAOLEUER: Oh, he lives in America, in Washington. I don't know what Washington looks like, maybe it looks like Bangkok. I've never been to Bangkok. He has two sons. His sons can't speak Hmong. They went to live in America a long time ago, they can only speak English.

My grandfather-general has five wives, but I have never seen them. I know one is Chinese and one is Laotian. The Chinese woman has two sons. I don't know about numbers three, four and five.

INTERVIEWER: Do you remember his name?

LAOLEUER: Oh, I must remember his name, he's an important man, a famous man. His name is Laobor Sewa. That's his Hmong name. I hope one day to see my grandfather come back to live in Laos.

CONDOMS - Somchai

Somchai, who is 26 years old and the deputy headman, is the official government health worker in the village. Every three months, when the mobile medical team of two doctors and two nurses come to the village from Chiangkhong hospital, Somchai sheds his Hmong clothes and dons a neat white shirt and black trousers to act as health worker, village pharmacist and interpreter. His family was one of the original seven to move to Kiew Khan twenty years ago.

SOMCHAI: In my life I haven't done much work in the fields. My parents were quite rich for Hmong people. When I was young, I went to study in Nakhon Sawan Province. I was there for ten years. For five years after leaving school, I had nothing to do. Sometimes when some people in the village were ill, and if they couldn't speak Thai very well, they would ask me to go with them to the hospital in Chiangkhong. The people at the hospital began to get to know me.

A year later, the villagers and a government official chose me to work for the government to help the people in the village. I had a boss in Chiangsaen who taught me how to give medicine to the people. Sometimes if someone was ill, I would have to tell them to go to the hospital. They didn't have to pay the hospital, they had a piece of paper from my boss to show at the hospital. The people were very poor and had no money.

Most people didn't like to take medicine to stop them having babies. A lot of my work was to explain to the people how to take the pill and how to use condoms.

My biggest problem was with the condom. Oh, I wish I'd had a picture-book to help me to explain to the people how to use them. I put the condom on my finger and told them they must use it when they make love to a woman. Hmong people don't know anything, really they don't. When they wanted to sleep with their wives, they put the condoms on their fingers and then made love. Then after two or three months they'd come back to me to complain that I'd given them bad medicine. They complained that their wives were pregnant.

I had to explain two different things to them. I had to explain how to use the condom and how to take the pill. With the pill, I forgot to tell them that the pill was only for the woman and not for the man. Most Hmong women cannot speak Thai and are too shy to talk about sex, or even just to come and listen. Mostly it was the men who came to see the doctor, but the doctor couldn't speak Hmong. Sometimes I was too busy and forgot to translate what the doctor had said. The men were too shy to ask when they didn't understand.

When they came back to complain, I had to figure out what they had done wrong. I asked them about when their wives took the medicine, whether it was every morning or in the evening. And I asked them about how many pills their wives took in one day. They answered that not only the women took the pills but also the men. They said, "Why does only my wife take the medicine? I make love to her, so, of course I must also take the medicine. It is me giving the seed". That is what they thought.

I made a very big mistake. I forgot to tell them whether it was the man or the woman who had to take the pill. So in every thirty day period, they ran out of the pills after only fifteen days.

I am married now. I have no problems. My wife was very young when I married her, only fourteen years old. I have one son. Since the school was built and many more people have begun to learn Thai, we have had fewer problems with medicine. Many children can now speak Thai. The doctors come from the hospital to show the people how to use the condom and how to take the pill. They use a film to help explain. Hmong people like watching the film. Everybody laughs, it is a lot better now. But because of the misunderstandings before, we have many childen in the village. Some families have eight children and only the parents and maybe the first child can work in the fields.

FINDING A BRIDE - Somchai

Somchai (see Condoms) married two years ago when he was 24 years old and his wife 14 years old. They have one son.

INTERVIEWER: How do the Hmong mariage customs differ from those of the Thai? How important is marriage to the Hmong people?

SOMCHAI: Often we don't have a big party or celebration but marriage is important to us.

Girls and boys have a good opportunity to meet each other during the New Year. Many men come to the village from other villages to see the girls and to look for a wife. Hmong New Year used to be on January the first, but now because of the changing weather we often finish the work in the fields earlier and so we are able to have the celebration earlier. We have to have a lot of rice and vegetables for New Year. Girls and boys can meet each other during New Year. After the end of the celebration, the boy can ask the girl to come and live with his family. He also has to ask her parents. Later, when they have some money, a pig or two, some chickens and some whisky, the boy gives a party. Some boys and girls live together for a few years, have one or two children, and then when they have enough money, they have the wedding.

The other way is not so good. If the boy is not good-looking, but the girl is good-looking, it can be difficult for the boy to ask the girl to go and live with his family. It's also difficult for him to ask the girl's parents for their permission. If the boy doesn't want to ask her, he then asks a friend to help him in forcing the girl to go to his house. The boy drags her to his house. The girl's parents usually hear the noise and follow them carrying big sticks. The parents hit the boy and his friend over the head. But that's all, they don't do anything serious, they just use the big sticks.

The boy's friend helps to talk to the girl's parents. The boy usually promises that he wants to marry the girl because she is a good girl and promises to look after her. Then he gives them some money. Then the parents agree. But this other way is not so common now, really it is more from the past. Now if a man forces the girl, she might try and kill herself by eating opium. Women are different now.

The usual way is better. After the boy and girl meet, and if they like each other, the boy can visit the girl's house in the middle of the night after the parents have gone to bed. If the girl likes him, they can sleep together. If she doesn't like him, she can tell him to go away. They can sleep together many times. If later either of them changes their minds, they can break off the relationship. It's usually the boy who decides whether to stop or to carry on. If the girl gets pregnant, they can't stop, they must get married. If the boy refuses to get married, he must give the girl some money to help look after the baby. But when this happens, the girl and her parents are usually unhappy.

For most Hmong families, the daughter must marry and go away to live with her husband's family. Her parents can't look after her all their lives. Even when the boyfriend has no money, nothing, they still let her go.

FIRST LOVE - Namai

Namai is 23 years old and is married with one child. She was born in Laos and at one time lived in Ban Gay refugee camp near Chingkhong. She now lives in Kiew Khan. She spends most of her time working in the fields.

INTERVIEWER: You must have been good-looking when you were still a young, single girl.

NAMAI: I don't know. When I was a girl, many people told me I was better looking than other girls.

INTERVIEWER: Did many boys come to visit you?

NAMAI: Yes, many men came to visit me every day. When they came, they came with radios. They wanted to let me listen to the radios. In the past, if a man wanted a girl to be his girlfriend, he would take his radio with him when he went to see the girl. Sometimes the men would show off by playing Thai music. In the past, if someone had a radio, even a cheap one, they tried to show off a little bit. The people in the village thought that anybody with a radio must be from a rich family. In the past, there were no cars or motorbikes. If you wanted to go somewhere, you had to walk or go by horse. The road was very bad. There was no school. Radios were special.

INTERVIEWER: Which man were you interested in?

NAMAI: (Giggles) I'm too shy, I can't tell you that. I'm too embarrassed to talk about my past. My husband is not happy when he hears about my past, but...okay then, it was Sompat, he's the one. I liked him a lot and he liked me a lot. Sompat was quite good-looking, he looked smart and he went to a Thai school in the town. He was cleverer than the other men. He had many nice shirts and shoes. His skin was almost white.

INTERVIEWER: Why didn't you marry Sompat? What happened?

NAMAI: I liked Sompat for a year. We made plans to get married. But before getting married, he had to finish school. We were both eighteen years old. His parents didn't like me because they wanted him to finish school first and then to marry another girl, not me. His parents were richer than mine.

One day he came to tell me that his parents had told him to go back to school, to go back to finish school. But Sompat wouldn't listen to his parents. He was angry with them. He came to live in my house for a while.

My parents didn't like him. They had problems because Sompat's parents tried to make them feel inferior. My parents were poor. Sompat made it difficult for me. At night, I had to sleep in my cousin's house. Then Sompat got angry with me.

A little bit later his father told me to stop the relationship with Sompat. He wanted me to tell Sompat to go back to school. So I told Sompat to return to school. But he wouldn't listen. He didn't want to go back.

One night I went to my cousin's house to sleep. Sompat came to see me at my parent's house. My mother told him I had gone to Chiangkham. Sompat didn't believe her. He knew my mother didn't like him and was telling him a lie.

Later that night, he came to me at my cousin's house. He called on me to open the door for him. He said he had something to tell me. I was in the room and answered him. I said I didn't want to talk to him. In my heart, I was very upset, I was just pretending not to want to see him. I had to say that because his father had told me to stop the relationship, to finish everything. His father had told me that if I liked Sompat, I must stop seeing him.

So I told Sompat that I was soon to be married and that he must go back to school. I told him we had to finish everything. Sompat cried a lot. He told me he loved me a lot and that he wanted to marry me. He didn't want me to marry anybody else. He really cried.

I didn't open the door to him. He cried and became angry. I had told him I was soon to marry. He thought I had never liked him. He was very upset. He thought I was speaking the truth and not just pretending. Then he broke down the door. He came into the room and hit me. He hit me because he was so upset. He thought I was going to marry someone else.

I still loved him and wanted him. It was difficult to explain what I felt. He hit me by mistake. I understood. I was not angry with him.

MARRIED TO A THAI BOY - Nayua

Nayua is 15 years old and has recently left the village to live with her young man a few kilometres away down the mountain. She still works hard on her father's land near her new house. She has discovered that life as a poor lowlander can be just as hard as that of a Hmong. Her boyfriend is a house builder and intends having his future children raised as Hmong for their first five years, and after that, as Thais.

INTERVIEWER: Do you like living with Thais? Is it fun?

NAYUA: Yes, it's fun. I live with my boyfriend and his two cousins. Sometimes he takes me to see his parents. They are very nice. They buy me sweets. They are Thai and I am the daughter-in-law. I don't work too hard. On the mountain I used to work hard the whole year. Even during the rains, we didn't have a holiday. When it was hot, we still had to work. And we still worked when it was very cold. Living here on the farm is better. My boyfriend's parents bought us some chickens, and ducks and sheep. We have chicken meat and eggs to eat. Oh, living down in the valley is best. I don't need to walk far to look for firewood. It's easy to go to the Thai villages. And we have bicycles.

INTERVIEWER: Do you have any problems living with your boyfriend?

NAYUA: Yes, of course. Sometimes when we talk together, we can't understand each other. Sometimes I am angry and say bad things to him in Hmong. He doesn't understand it. But when he's angry with me, and says bad things to me, I understand what he says.

INTERVIEWER: Do you often go to his parent's house?

NAYUA: Oh yes, twice a week. They are good people. But...but...Hmong people can live together even though they are not married, but, but we do not drink whisky and have parties all the time. Is it the same with farang?

INTERVIEWER: Yes, the same. Do his parents mind you not being married?

NAYUA: I think they understand.

INTERVIEWER: Do your parents-in-law like Hmong clothes?

NAYUA: Oh no, neither his parents nor him like Hmong clothes. His parents told me Hmong clothes aren't nice, aren't pretty. My boyfriend says I must wear Thai clothes now that I'm living off the mountain. If I go back to the mountain, I can wear my Hmong clothes again.

INTERVIEWER: Where did you meet your boyfriend?

NAYUA: My boyfriend came to cut some wood near my parent's fields. Every day we flirted together. Then he told me he loved me. I was embarrassed. He thought I loved him. He told his parents to ask my parents if I could live with him. My parents agreed.

INTERVIEWER: How long have you been living with your boyfriend?

NAYUA: We've been living together for nearly three months. Sometimes I think I want to go back to live with my parents up there. We're poor, but it's good fun at home.

INTERVIEWER: Does your sister also want to marry a Thai boy?

NAYUA: Namee doesn't want to marry yet. She prefers to be single. Sometimes I have tried to stop living with him. I've been angry many times. I don't know. I know only I don't...

STAYING SINGLE - Nadoa

Nadoa is 20 years old and single. She occasionally ventures out to the fields to work for the family but is usually to be found sitting outside her parent's house embroidering her clothes. Twenty is considerd old still to be single by Hmong standards but this doesn't bother Nadoa. She hopes she will never have to marry, but if she eventually has to, then she wants to delay the day as long as possible.

NADOA: I've seen my parents, and other families, and I'm sure I don't want to get married. If it's difficult for me, then I'll have to get married, but for me that's a terrible thing. I would age very quickly after one year of marriage. That's what is happening to all of my friends. One of my friends is the same age as me. Now she's got three children and looks very old, the same as an old woman of thirty-five. She has to work very hard in the fields and has to look after her children. She's always very busy. Now she's very thin. She has no time for herself. But anyway, I suppose she's still happy with her husband. Her husband isn't too bad.

INTERVIEWER: So you would rather not get married?

NADOA: For sure. If I were to marry, it wouldn't be for myself but for my parents. One reason I don't want to get married is because I have seen how many children my parents have. My mother has to work very hard. There's never enough money to buy food, never enough vegetables to eat. I am frightened of being married.

Some men are very nice when they first get married. Every day they help the wife with her work in the fields. But I see that after a woman has children, the husband doesn't take care of her. Even when she's pregnant, and wants to eat something, and she tells her husband to go and buy something for her, he never listens to the wife. She has to cry.

I remember my friend when she was pregnant, she was unwell and very thin. She couldn't eat anything and was sick every day. She had never drunk coffee before and suddenly wanted to try it. She couldn't stop thinking about coffee. She had heard that farang drink it for breakfast. She wanted to see how different it was from Chinese tea.

She didn't know how to make it, how to cook it. She had only heard of coffee. She asked her husband to buy some for her in Chiangkhong. Her husband knew the word for coffee, and he could read "coffee" in Thai. He went to Chiangkhong but he spent the money on his lunch. He didn't buy the coffee for her. So she came to my house to ask me to help her ask you and Jon for some coffee. Do you remember? Her husband wouldn't help her.

Now her stomach is big. Bad luck for the baby if it's born a girl. Unlucky until her death. I have seen women after they get married, they look different from before. They are not pretty. They lose their looks.

Women have to carry the children everywhere. Even when the woman goes to the town to buy or sell something, she has to take her baby with her. But the men can go anywhere they want. They don't care what the women think of them. They don't care if the women are not happy.

The men aren't interested in the women at home. They think they have bought the women for work. Some Hmong men are already married and have two or three children but they still go and flirt with girls. They don't care what the wife thinks. If she complains too much, or even only a little bit, the man will tell her to go, to get out and leave the children with him. Or sometimes the man would say that he did all the work when they first got married, that they have a house and farm because of the man's work in the past, and that if the woman doesn't do all the work now, then she can get out and leave the house.

INTERVIEWER: What do you think about your parents?

NADOA: Father and mother? The only good thing they can do is to produce children. They have many children, a full house. They have no idea about herbal medicine. I don't like having so many brothers and sisters. In our family only a few people work very hard. My mother and me, we work very hard in the corn fields, but when we sell the crop it is always my father who gets the money. He always has gambling debts to pay off.

I've seen many bad things so I don't want to get married. I don't want to have to work until I die. If I help my mother in the fields, then I think we should have the money, some for my mother and me, and some for my younger brothers and sisters, and not only my father. I don't want to work if he gets all the money.

If I were to marry, I'd have to have children. I'd have no time for myself. My parents are poor, better if I work for my mother and brothers and sisters. Every day if I want to work, I do, if I don't want to work, I don't. Nobody complains.

MOVING IN WITH THE IN-LAWS - Nalee

Nalee is about 21 years old and comes from the Hmong village of Ban Giang, near Chiangkhong. She moved to Kiew Khan three or four years ago after marrying a local man. She has one child and is considered by her father-in-law to be a hard worker and a great asset to the family.

NALEE: I originally came from Ban Giang in Chiangkhong district.

INTERVIEWER: How did you come to be living in Kiew Khan?

NALEE: I got married. My husband and parents-in-law asked my parents to bring me to live with the family in Kiew Khan. It has now been about three years since I came to them to work in the fields. My parents-in-law have a farm. I help them work in the fields and on the farm. We plant cassava, corn and rice.

If my parents-in-law have any extra money, and meat and whisky after selling the crops, they send some to my mother and father in Ban Giang, so that I can stay here with my husband's family for longer.

If my parents-in-law haven't got any money, meat and whisky to send to my parents, then my parents will ask me to live with them again and to help them by working on their farm and in their fields.

LITTLE GIRL - Namai

Namai is 4 years old and is a rather naughty, but a really very nice, little girl. She spends much of her time with her youngest brother Namor, whom she carries on her back wherever she goes. She tries to avoid too much contact with her younger brother Sheng because she is fed up with Sheng's constant crying. Since the last Hmong New Year celebration she has started wearing her clothes, because, she explains, she feels she is now becoming a woman.

NAMAI : After New Year my friends seem different. Some like to act bigger, they like to be like women, I don't know, but Bor likes to tell me to do things, she likes to be like my mother. Now Bor doesn't like to play with boys. Now I don't like shouting with anybody at home. I like to get up early and try and get away from home as soon as I can. I don't like playing with Sheng. He's boring, he always cries. When I hear him cry, I get cross. I like to play with girls rather than with boys.

INTERVIEWER: What games do you play with your friends?

NAMAI: Sometimes I like to play cooking with mud. I like to be Najia and I like my friend to be Jon. Jon has to carry the water for Najia for cooking. Sometimes I like to play that I am my big sister at night. I pretend boys come to see me. We play many different things.

One of my friends likes to play building a house with leaves, and being married with two or three children.

Since New Year I now like the clothes my mother made for me. I like to wear my new shirt. Now if I have no clothes on, I feel shy because Bor has clothes on every day. I want more clothes.

SCHOOL LEAVER - Nabai

Nabai is 11 years old and is one of eight children. Her days are usually spent in the fields tending the crops, collecting wild vegetables, herbs and spices, or looking after the family's cows. She attended school in the village for two years before being told by her parents to work full-time in the fields for the family.

INTERVIEWER: Did you like going to school?

NABAI: Oh yes, I liked going to school very much. I started going to school before I could speak Thai. Every afternoon after school, I used to carry my little sister and go and play at my teacher's house. I used to help my teacher by doing little jobs. My teacher liked to speak Thai with me. I can speak Thai better than any of my friends even though I went to school for only two years.

At my school, we have five different classes. There are sixty-eight pupils and four teachers. The teachers teach us everything. Twice a week we eat lunch at school. Our teachers cook the food for us, but we also help a little bit. We have chicken, vegetables and pork for our meals. Delicious. At home we don't often eat good food. We only eat meat at home when someone in the family is ill, or when it's New Year. Sometimes we make offerings of meat to the spirits. During our New Year celebration, my parents prepare meat with salt and put it in a jar to keep it for a long time.

Children like to eat at school a lot. Before, we used to have milk at school, that's why we liked to go there. I liked to go but my parents told me to stop going. It's a pity but I must help my parents. I must look after my brothers and sisters.

INTERVIEWER: What do you do now?

NABAI: I have to look after my brothers and sisters, the little ones, altogether four of them. I have to tell them to wash before my parents come home, and I must cook rice and look after the cows and sheep, and find wood for the fire.

INTERVIEWER : Do the teachers at your school ever hit the children? Did your teacher ever hit you?

NABAI: Never. He usually only hit the boys and I don't like to play with boys. Sometimes at school, I only had a little time to play after lunch because my friends and I had to do our embroidery. I have to have my embroidery with me at all times. My mother says it's better not to play, better to work, because Hmong clothes take a long time to finish. During New Year, we Hmong must wear new clothes. Everyone must be well dressed. My sister has nice clothes and a nice silver neckring that my grandfather gave to her. When I see it, I am very jealous of my big sister. If I was the first daughter, my father would give me one. I think when I am fifteen years old and a woman, my father will give me one.

Now I still want to go to school. When my parents told me that I couldn't go to school any more, I was a little bit sad. I can read and write just a little bit. I still remember my teacher's name, it is Suwit. And I still remember his wife and son.

INTERVIEWER: Do the boys and girls learn together at your school?

NABAI: Girls and boys learn together. Some pupils at my school leave Kiew Khan and go to school in Pitsanulok Province. Many Hmong people live in Pitsanulok Province. It is very far from our village, so only some of the boys go. The girls have no chance to go. The girls have to help their parents.

INTERVIEWER: When you were still at school, did you ever think about what you would like to do when you finished school?

NABAI: Oh yes, I wanted to be a doctor. I have seen the doctors that come to our village. They look so neat and clean in their white clothes. They look very respectable. I would like that a lot.

INTERVIEWER: What do you look forward to now?

NABAI: Hmong New Year. I like Hmong New Year very much. It's good fun. If my parents have some money from selling corn and rice, they take us to visit other villages. For New Year we have bull fighting, horse racing and dancing. Boys from other villages come to court the girls at our village. I look forward to Hmong New Year very much.

I would like to ask my mother to let me visit another town, after all, I am eleven now. Chiang Mai, Chiang Rai, what do they look like? I don't know, I've never been to them. I have only been to Chiangkhong, and once to Chiangsaen during Thai New Year last year. At Chiangsaen everybody was looking at us. We were very embarrassed because we were wearing different clothes. I would like to try wearing Thai clothes but am too shy of what my friends would think.

INTERVIEWER: What do you think about the young Thai men who come to the village to court Hmong girls.?

NABAI: They look rich. They have motorbikes.

INTERVIEWER: Later, when you are a woman, will you marry a Hmong man or a Thai?

NABAI: I don't know, maybe a Thai.

HUNTING - Laojongser

Laojongser is 42 years old, married with a family, and is a hunter. When not out in the jungle hunting boar or deer, he helps his wife in the fields. One of his sons goes to school in Chiangsaen. Laojongser hopes that one day this son will eventually be able to go to university.

LAOJONGSER: Hunting is very varied. Early in the morning when there is no rain, the people in the village go to the fields. They have to walk quite far. Sometimes they see tracks made by big animals. Everybody is experienced at recognising animal tracks. When they see the tracks, they come back to the village to tell the hunters. Then the hunters get their guns, and some plain rice, salt and chillies and go out to follow the tracks.

Sometimes the hunters have to follow the animals very far, until the animals are tired from being followed and not being able to stop and eat. Sometimes the animals can't eat for three or four days. They get very tired and can't walk properly and have to stop for a while in an area of thick jungle.

The hunters know where the animals are, they know the animals are tired. They can see that the tracks go into the thicker jungle and then stop. The hunters, many people, split up and stand around the area where the animals are. Then they send in the dogs. the dogs bark and frighten the animals and make them run from cover.

The person who shoots and kills the animal keeps the head and half the body. All the rest of the hunters share the other half. Sometimes there are ten or fifteen people who have to share.

In the past we preferred to go hunting in big groups. Sometimes we caught many animals. We had to share, to share everything. When we hunt in big groups, we always have one person to be the leader. He's usually quite old. He has to be clever, he has to make the plans. He tells the other hunters where to stand.

If a person moves when they are waiting for the animal to break from cover, and the animal goes towards him, and he shoots and misses, then that person has to pay a fine. If you miss your chance to kill the animal, you are fined a pig. If you do not have a pig, you have to give a chicken.

Now I prefer to go alone. If I want to go hunting, I go, if I don't want to go, I don't. I know I am a good hunter. When I get animals, the size doesn't matter. I can keep everything myself. I don't have to share with other people. I don't care if I shoot and miss.

It is quiet difficult to go alone, but I have good experience. But it is dangerous to go alone if you are not a good hunter. You have to be very, very careful in the jungle.

INTERVIEWER: How do you know where the pigs and deer will be? How do you get them if they are hiding in thick jungle and you are just one person?

LAOJONGSER: If I go alone, I don't have to stand by the thick jungle waiting. I know which places are good. I know which places the animals like to come looking for food. I always check before I go hunting. I make sure that there are animal tracks and droppings, and I look to see if the grass is disturbed. Then I make a hide in a tree. It's easy to see the animals from the tree. It's also easy to shoot them.

The boars and deer mostly come from across the river in Laos. There is a lot of jungle near the border, especially at Huai Tu, Huai Sa and Huai Sai Man villages. The animals like to cross the river at an easy place and then go straight to Doi Luang. At Doi Luang I know where to catch them.

INTERVIEWER: Do you remember how many animals you have caught since you first started hunting?

LAOJONGSER: I can't remember how many in the last thirty years, but I've caught about thirty or forty deer in the last two or three years, and many boars and spotted cats and others.

INTERVIEWER: How big are the boars and deer?

LAOJONGSER: A boar hog is quite big, his teeth can be eight centimetres long. Some of the deer are very big, bigger than a man. Sometimes they are dangerous to catch. It can be difficult to see the boars if you are inexperienced. Then it is very dangerous.

It is best to build a small tree-house high up in a tree. People smell differently from animals. The animals are careful all the time. Wild animals are experienced with people. If you sit on the ground in the same area as an animal, or if there is a slight wind, the animal can smell you. Their nose is better than ours. The animals know it is not safe for them and run away.

They have to be careful at all times.

Sometimes a person shoots a boar but doesn't kill it, it's still alive and not dead. It's in a lot of pain. Then the boar has to especialy careful. If it smells a person, it turns to attack. It has to attack because it can't run away.

Animals can see people at night because their eyes are very strong. So I always wait up the tree where it's safer and easier to see the animals. Once a boar attacked some people. It was quite serious. And my brother was once attacked and very seriously injured. He had to stay in the hospital for many days.

INTERVIEWER: What do you do if you are sitting up a tree with just your one musket and you see two or three boars?

LAOJONGSER: If there are two or three, I choose the biggest and shoot it. Then if I have time, I try and shoot a second one. Then I climb down to make sure they are dead. Sometimes they are not killed straight off, they run to the jungle. I follow them, but only if it is daytime. At night, I can only shoot one boar because it's difficult to see. I have to shine a torch into the the animal's eyes.

Usually if there are two or three animals, they are from the same family - a sow and her litter. If the piglets are very young, they usually get frightened after I shoot their mother and run away to hide for a while. When they feel better, they return to see their mother, to see what happened to her. I wait for the piglets to come back and then I shoot them. Sometimes I try to catch them alive.

INTERVIEWER: When is the best season for hunting?

LAOJONGSER: The season is not too important. I can go hunting all-year-round. But I prefer it when there is no rain. It is easier when there is no rain. When the rains have just started, it is still a good time, and also during the cold season when the weather is lovely, when it is easy to walk, neither too wet nor too hot. There are a lot of animals in the wet season but I'm too lazy to go. It's too wet and cold, and too difficult to walk. I usually do other things in the rainy season. I help my family to work in the maize, rice and cassava fields.

In the winter, the best time to get the pigs is usually at about four o'clock in the afternoon, or early in the morning at about seven or eight. In the cold season, the animals are cold and come out into the sunshine.

INTERVIEWER: How did you first become a hunter?

LAOJONGSER: When I was twelve, my elder brother liked to hunt. He wasn't a very good hunter. I liked to go with him for fun. I really wanted to be a hunter. I went with my brother to learn how to hunt. I learned very quickly. I became a better hunter than my brother. When I was twelve, I used to go with a big group, but for many years now I've always made sure I've gone alone. I've been going on my own now for thirty years.

I have my father's gun. He bought it from some Yao people. He paid for it with silver coins, not with Thai money. It was very expensive. It cost thirty-two haeng. That's about one hundred thousand baht in today's Thai money.

INTERVIEWER: Are you never afraid when you go hunting alone?

LAOJONGSER: No, I like to go alone. It's easier to walk when I'm alone. I have to be careful all the time. But I don't have to worry about accidents with guns. If I were to go with a group, I would have to be careful about accidents all the time. There are many vines and creepers in the jungle. Sometimes when you are walking, it's possible for a creeper to catch on the trigger and fire the gun by accident. The people walking in front or behind can be shot by mistake. People have to be careful when walking along a small track with very old guns, home-made guns, because the guns don't have safety catches.

INTERVIEWER: What do you do with the meat you get from hunting?

LAOJONGSER: In the past, I used to get meat just for the family to eat because I didn't know how to sell it. Hill people used to have no idea about buying and selling. We used to keep it for our family and relatives. But now when I get something, I sell some of the meat and keep some. I buy bullets with the money I get from selling some of the meat. A long time ago we didn't buy the bullets, we made them ourselves. I used to make them. Or sometimes my family did. But it's difficult to make them.

Sometimes when I go hunting, I find tracks of a deer or boar and follow them, sometimes for three or four days. I follow them until I get the animal. I get very tired but I enjoy myself.

THE SPIRITS OF THE BOAR AND GUN - Laojongser

> *Laojongser (see Hunting) devotes much of his energies to hunting. He attributes his many successes to his long experience and skill and also to his careful observance of the spirit rituals.*

LAOJONGSER: Come to my house, sit, sit. Do you want to eat? Today I am eating wild boar from last night. I went hunting and got a sow and two piglets. Three pigs altogether.

INTERVIEWER: Really! How big? Are you about to eat now or do you first have to make an offering to the spirits?

LAOJONGSER: Of course we have to make an offering to the spirits first. I did it this morning. If we do not make an offering to them, then nobody can eat the meat. I will tell you about it while we are eating.

After we get back home, the first thing we must do is to cut the head off the body. Then we cook a small portion from the body for the spirits of the boar and the spirits of the gun. The boar and gun spirits are so important. Good and bad depend on the spirits.

We have to get some white paper, incense and also cooked meat from the boar, and rice and drinking water. I put everything with the gun and the boar's head on the floor just inside the door. Then I invite a village elder who knows about spirits to come and tell the spirits, the pig's spirits, "It is your meat that we are eating, and we burn the white paper for you." If it is a big boar, we must burn a big piece of paper, if a small one, then we burn a smaller piece of paper.

Then I must say to the boar's spirit, "Excuse me for killing you. Do not remember that it was I who killed you, forget everything that happened today."

Then I must say to the spirit of the gun, "Last night you shot a boar, today we eat the meat of the pig from last night. I have to eat, you have to eat. Next time if we go hunting and you see a wild boar, make sure it is a boar. If you see a person, make sure it is a person. Do not kill by mistake. Do not kill by accident. If you see a pig, shoot the pig and make sure the pig is dead. If you go off by accident, do not hit anything."

INTERVIEWER: If you go hunting and kill an animal and you do not make an offering to the spirits, do the spirits do anything bad to you or your family?

LAOJONGSER: If the spirits cannot eat, nobody can eat. It is a Hmong tradition that you make offerings to the spirits every time you get something. If somebody thinks the spirits are not too important and he doesn't give anything to the spirits, then the spirits will do something bad to him the next time he goes hunting.

INTERVIEWER: Are there lucky and unlucky days for hunting?

LAOJONGSER: In the past, hunters had to check the day to see if it was a good day or a bad one for hunting. There were special old men to check the days. Now it is not too important. It is important only to make offerings to the spirits of the boar and gun. It is very important to make offerings to the spirits.

HUNTING ACCIDENT - Laojongser

Laojongser (see Hunting / The Spirits of the Boar and Gun) never joins a group of hunters on a hunting expedition, and rarely goes out with even a single companion. One of the reasons for this is his fear of a shooting accident.

INTERVIEWER: Has anybody ever been shot by mistake whilst hunting?

LAOJONGSER: In the past, when I lived in my old village at Doi Luang, a friend came to ask me to go hunting with him. I couldn't go that day. It was strange, that day something in my head told me that I shouldn't go with him. I felt sad inside but I didn't know why. My friend went alone.

I remember it was the cold season and there were many boars coming to the maize fields to eat there. One man, the owner of a field, knew there were many wild pigs coming to his fields. He went home to get his gun to shoot the boars.

At the same time, my friend, who was not an experienced hunter, went to the maize fields to wait for a boar. Then the owner returned with his gun. He didn't know there was already someone waiting to shoot the pigs. They didn't know about each other.

The owner heard a noise. He heard some boars fighting each other. At the same time, my friend moved his body. When he moved, he knocked against a tree or bush. The owner of the maize field was waiting to shoot. He thought the bush moved because the pigs were fighting underneath. But under the bush was a person, not a pig. He shot my friend by mistake.

The owner heard somebody make a noise and then tell him not to shoot again because he was there. The owner ran to see him. He was nearly dead. The owner carried my friend, who was nearly dead, back to the road. He left him on the road and ran back to the village to get some people to help him carry the wounded man.

In those days there were no cars. If somebody was ill and had to go to hospital, they had to go by government helicopter.

My friend stayed in the hospital in Chiangkhong for two days. The bullet had hit him in the face and mouth, he couldn't speak. Then he died.

MY HUSBAND - THREE TELLING STORIES - Najor

Najor is 41 years old, married to Laoter, and has eight children. She works hard in the fields to make ends meet, and often sleeps with her three youngest children in the family's small field-house in order to avoid wasting time walking to and from the fields. The family is kept poor by her husband's constant gambling losses. Laoter is a member of the Thai Border Patrol Police and is stationed in the village. His nine hundred baht a month salary rarely finds its way into the family purse.

NAJOR: In the past, I lived at Doi Luang village. My husband was a soldier there. We moved down the mountain when the road was built to Kiew Khan. At that time, I had only Anu and Nachu. I was three months pregnant with Nabai. I don't know why, but I was very ill with my third child. I had a fever right up until I gave birth. I was very thin but I still had to work in the fields. Laoter never looked after me. He never bought me anything to eat. He earned nine hundred baht a month from the army and got free food and accommodation. He worked fifteen days on and fifteen days off. While working, he stayed at the army camp, sometimes he went to Chiangkhong.

THE PRETTY HMONG GIRL

He once took a Hmong girl from Kiew Khan shopping in Chiangkhong. He bought her a Yao turban, it cost one hundred and eighty baht, so much money in those days. The Hmong girl was very pretty, but only her face, not her heart. She liked to sleep with many different men, any man who had enough money to buy her a present. Because she was so beautiful, many men liked to flirt with her, including married men with children.

I don't know what happened but I think one day the sky spirit must have done a bad thing to her. She had gone to live at Pa-mon village. When she came back to the village to visit some friends, I was really shocked. Before she had been so pretty, but now she was so ugly. She was almost blind, and she had a big scar on her face. No man wanted to look at her. She was very sad and started to smoke opium. She smoked a lot and got thinner and thinner. There was nothing beautiful about her any more.

In the past, Laogwa and Laolao were soldiers, but they were good men. When they got the day off, they went to see their families. On pay-day they bought food and material for their families. They didn't gamble. But Laoter, my husband, he started gambling from the very first day he joined the army. The gambling spirit lives in his heart and in his head. He would sell anything for money for gambling. In the past, I had eighteen cows. They were my wedding present from my parents. Now he has sold most of them. He only takes, he never gives. Sometimes I am very sad at what he does.

THE BIG LIZARD

Once he went hunting and caught a big lizard. On the way back home he stopped in his friend's field to cook the lizard. His friend was Lahu, from Huai Sa village. On the same day my mother went to some nearby fields. She saw Laoter and went up to him. He didn't offer any lizard to my mother. She didn't mind, she thought it was better to keep it for the family. But after he finished eating half of the lizard, he took the other half and gave it to his friend for his friend's family in Huai Sa.

My mother had already returned to Kiew and told me that he had a big lizard. When he came home and my son and daughter saw him, they were very happy. They were happy to see their father and happy because they thought they could eat lizard meat. The children ran up to him and asked him how big it was, and how to cook it. I was in the bedroom. I opened the door to see him and to see how big the lizard was. I saw nothing. I asked him where the lizard meat was. He shouted at me and the children. He looked very angry. He shouted to the children, " I have eaten lizard, not elephant." He made up an excuse. He has no heart.

In the past, when we had our wedding celebration, his parents didn't help him to pay the dowry. The money he paid to my parents so that he could marry me was not only his money. I had to work very hard to help him pay. We had to get the money from selling the crops. In the past, when we were first starting to raise a family, I worked very hard to make money because I wanted to have a good life. His brother looked down on me because his brother was rich. He had over thirty cows. I wanted my husband and I to be rich.

A SECOND WIFE

Three years ago he took a Lahu girl to be a second wife. He took her to live with him at the army post on top of the hill. Nobody told me. It was strange because for over one month he didn't come to see the family. His friends didn't tell me. But the wife of one of them told me, she felt sorry for me and my children.

One night, at about nine o'clock, I went up the hill to see him. I took a big stick with me. I went straight to his hut. I opened the door and went to hit the Lahu girl, twice, quite hard. I wanted to hit her until she died. I was standing by the door, so she couldn't get out. She climbed up the wall to the roof.

I thought my husband would help me. I thought he would ask to be forgiven and try and be friendly with me. After all, he had done the big thing wrong. But he did the opposite. He punched me and kicked me. I was surprised and very upset.

Later I told him I would contact the police in Chiangkhong, but his boss said we had to clear everything up that night. I knew the boss soldier had a secret Lahu wife, and that he was worried that he might get the sack if his superiors heard about it, because his Lahu wife was from a refugee camp. You know, if someone lives in a refugee camp, they can't go anywhere, they have to stay in the camp. I had to do what the boss soldier said because he was quite nice to me. But Laoter didn't want to discuss it.

After two days, my husband came to say sorry. He was very polite and friendly. I told him I wanted to divorce him. He said I could go if I wanted to, but he said I had to leave my children. I agreed. I went back to my parents' house. But my parents didn't like the idea. My father told me everything in my house belonged to me. He said Laoter was in the wrong, so Laoter had to leave the house, not me. So I went back and told Laoter to leave. But my children didn't like it. They cried a lot. Even though he was a bad father, the children still wanted him.

Even now after so many years he is still bad. I think, if in the past I could have seen into the future, I wouldn't have married Laoter.

THE FIRST FARANG - Somchai

Somchai (see Condoms / Finding A Bride) is always ready to welcome a farang into his house, but speaking no English, he sometimes feels frustrated at his inability to communicate.

SOMCHAI: About three years ago, I first met a farang. In the past no cars or minibuses could come to the village because of the bad road and the high mountains. It was difficult for farang to come. The ones that did manage to come always came by motorbike. They were always so dirty from the bad road. I felt sorry for them. The road was very dusty, there were many accidents. Farang countries have clean roads, I have seen it on television in Nakhon Sawan.

I used to be frightened of farang. Farang have big bodies and are so different from Thais. I thought maybe farang were dangerous. But after a few farang tried to talk to me and were friendly, I was not so frightened of farang. I feel I like them.

Their bodies look very clean, their hair is different and they are very tall, so very different from Hmong. I would like to be big. If I was as big as a farang, I think I would be very strong and could work very hard.

But sometimes the children here at Kiew Khan village start crying and run away when they see a farang get out of a minibus, or off a motorbike. If the farang give sweets and smile, the children are not so frightened. They like the farang to take photographs of them, they like it very much.

Also the women like having their photograph taken, they like to see themselves on paper. But most women are too shy and think they are not beautiful enough to have their pictures taken. Or sometimes the women think their clothes are too dirty. Sometimes the girls run off to put on their best clothes.

INTERVIEWER: Has a farang ever taken a picture of you and your wife?

SOMCHAI: Never has a farang taken a photograph of me or my family. I would like to have it done some time.

OLD WOMAN - Maethao

Maethao is 86 years old and lives with her only son and his family of twenty-two. Like many of the older people in Kiew Khan she only speaks the Hmong language, and considers herself too old to learn Thai. She spends her days chatting to the other old people, looking after her many grandchildren, and helping her son's two wives to run the household.

INTERVIEWER: Maethao, how long ago was it that you first saw a farang?

MAETHAO: Oh, I can't remember how long. I think it must have been about thirty years ago. There were farang at Doi Luang Prae Muang, oh, a long time ago. They came to build a place for the helicopters to land at Doi Prae Muang. The farang I met before were very good people, they gave sweets to the children. Now farang never give anything to anyone.

INTERVIEWER: Mathao, what do you think of farang? Are they good-looking? Is there anything different about their bodies?

MAETHAO: Oh, oh, they are very good-looking. Farang are good-looking, they have nice noses. Most farang I see have a nice body. Hardly ever is a farang not good-looking. I like farang.

CHAPTER FIVE
LISU

1) **Village Patriarch** - Ja-pu'er, 87.
   The story of Ja-pu'er, forty years a headman, village founder, and grandfather to one hundred and fifty.

2) **The Second World War Comes to the Hills** - Ja-pu'er, 87.
   Ja-pu'er's memories of the war and the Japanese.

3) **Lisu New Year** - Ali-ya, 18.
   A time for finding a boyfriend and showing respect to your elders.

4) **Buddhist, Not Christian** - Nakalae, 15.
   Nakalae describes how Chinese Christians try and convert the Buddhist villagers to Christianity.

5) **Schoolboy** - Chatchai Bandu, 13.
   Chat-chai tells of the problems he and the other village children face in going to the local Thai school.

6) **Cow Girl** - Nakasae, 14.
   Nakasae relates how she is happy to take out the cows every day and feels no need to go to school.

7) **A Woman's Life** - Velawan, 26.
   Velawan describes the hardships and injustices of a hill tribe woman's life and describes how men "live off the women's sweat".

VILLAGE PATRIARCH - Ja-pu'er

Ja-pu'er is 87 years old and in very good health, although he does admit to less than perfect hearing. He was born in 1902 at Doi Chang, near Fang, in Chiangmai Province. His family was one of the very first Lisu families to settle in Thailand. He and his second wife, a Lahu woman, live with one of his sons and his son's family, in a large elevated house of timber planking. He was a headman for forty years and is the founder of Ja-pu'er village. For exercise he takes the family's cows out to graze.

INTERVIEWER: Goodmorning Khun Ja-pu'er. Today I'm lucky, you are at home. I've come many times before, but you were never at home. Did your wife tell you I wanted to ask you something? I want to ask you about your life.

JA-PU'ER: Oh, I've forgotten many things, (laughs). If I say something wrong, please excuse me. My ears are not good, but my eyes are still good. My eyes are much younger than my ears, oh, ha ha. Do you want to know about customs, culture, about my life in the fields or about my village? I know many things, come on, ask me.

INTERVIEWER: Your name is the same as the name of the village, and it is a Lahu name, but you are Lisu. Can you explain?

JA-PU'ER: Ja-pu'er is a Lahu name, But I am Lisu. My father was Lisu, my mother Shan. My parents used to live in Burma. At that time I don't know where I was, maybe I was the rain, or the wind or the soil (chuckles). My parents told me they came to make their home at Doi Chang. At Doi Chang there were Lahu, Lisu, Shans and Akha all living together.

My father and mother gave birth to me at Doi Chang. When I was in my early twenties, my parents moved the family down from the mountain to live in the hills near to where Ja-pu'er village now is. I am the founder of the first Ja-pu'er village. I cut down the forest and cleared the land around the village. In those days, we lived a little bit away from today's village. We had difficulties with building a bridge across the river. During the wet season, the river always flooded. Every year we had to rebuild the bridge. I got fed up with it. I had to cut the timber to build the bridge, it was very hard work. Sometimes when I wanted to leave the village, it was difficult to cross the river. It was especially dangerous for the children to cross the river when they had to go to school. I was the founder of the village, I was not happy, so I moved every family. We built a new village. Now we don't need to move anywhere again. Anyway, even if we wanted to move, there is nowhere to go now. Most people in the village are related to me. They gave my name to the village.

INTERVIEWER: How many wives, children and grandchildren do you have?

JA-PU'ER: Oh, ha ha, I can't remember exactly, ha ha, I think maybe two or three hundred. I've had two wives and fifteen children altogether, ha ha. Oh, from my fifteen children, there are now one hundred and fifty people. Some of my children had ten or fifteen children. A lot of children. From my one hundred and fifty grandchildren, you can get two or three hundred more children, ha ha. Have you ever seen the like before in Thailand?

My Thai name is Khun Saen Jai Muang. I think an official was having a joke with me when he gave me that name. Saen is Thai for one hundred thousand. In the future my grandsons can make one hundred thousand people, ha ha. My children and my grandchildren think I'm a great person.

I can't remember all of my two or three hundred grandchildren, I don't know who they all are. I remember my sons and daughters-in-law and some of the grandchildren, but most grandchildren I can't remember. Sometimes they bring me food, or they buy something for me, and I have to ask them which one of my sons is their father. Oh, too many grandchildren.

I was a headman for forty years. I was a Lisu-Lahu headman. My son became headman after me, and after him it will be one of my grandsons. Some of my grandsons have Thai surnames, they are the ones that went to school in the town. Some grandsons have finished college, some have studied, and some have been soldiers. One of them was a headteacher.

INTERVIEWER: Do you have any problems in your family because of its size? Do you have arguments?

JA-PU'ER: Certainly we have arguments. Some of my sons married Lahu women. Sometimes they have problems because of the different cultures. Lisu and Lahu are different. The men have to adopt the women's culture. Sometimes the men like Lisu clothes and don't like Lahu clothes. But the woman tell the men that if the men like Lisu clothes, then why didn't they marry a Lisu women? Why did they marry a Lahu women? They tell them that as they have married Lahu wives, the men also have to be Lahu. In the end the men have to agree.

The people can change during New Year, sometimes they are Lisu, sometimes they are Lahu. Lisu and Lahu New Year are at the same time. Every child who is half-and-half can wear Lisu clothes on some days. and Lahu clothes on others.

INTERVIEWER: Are any of your brothers and sisters still alive?

JA-PU'ER: My sister is still alive. She is ninety-nine years old. Now she is not quite all there. She plays with the children. Everyone in my family has a long life. My elder sister was one hundred and ten when she died.

INTERVIEWER: When did your parents die?

JA-PU'ER: Oh, maybe, er, oh, I have to think. Oh, I think my father died many years before my mother. I think my father was one hundred when he died. I was already a little bit old when my mother died. She was one hundred and twenty when she died. You know, old people when they are very old, they play just like children. They like to play with toys. My mother liked to play with cooking pots. She would forget everything.

Sometimes, after she had had a shower, she would come back to the house with no clothes on, just like a child. I think I will probably be the same when I am very old.

THE SECOND WORLD WAR COMES TO THE HILLS - Ja-pu'er

Ja-pu'er (see Village Patriarch) has experienced many things in his long and eventful life. He has been a silversmith and a blacksmith and at one time was a porter for the Thai army during the Second World War.

INTERVIEWER: What have you done in your life that is interesting?

JA-PU'ER: There have been many interesting things in my life. I used to be a silversmith, I used to play the Lahu musical pipes, and I was a blacksmith. In my long life I have seen may things. I have never been a soldier, but I have seen the two big wars, the wars in the whole world. In those days I was much younger and much stronger.

INTERVIEWER: Can you tell me about your experiences in the last big war?

JA-PU'ER: I think it was the people from the government who first warned us to be careful of the Japanese and farang soldiers who were fighting each other. The Japanese wanted to take Burma, but the farang soldiers fought better because they wanted to keep Burma for a colony. Many Japanese soldiers died in Burma and Thailand.

The headman, my father, told us that not many ordinary people would die from the fighting, but that daily life would be very hard. He said life would be very difficult. In the daytime, we would have to carry on with our normal work, but at night we wouldn't be able to sleep in our houses. He told the people that the war was nearly at an end, and that soon the soldiers would have to go back home. He said the Japanese soldiers would pass the village on their way back and that maybe they would steal from us and rape the girls.

INTERVIEWER: How difficult for you was the war? Were you frightened of the Japanese soldiers?

JA-PU'ER: The soldiers didn't kill ordinary people, they only wanted to kill soldiers and spies. Every man had to help the country in the war. I used to carry food and guns for the Thai soldiers.

The headman told everyone to dig a shelter. One for every family. It was like a house under the ground. The shelter was safer from the bombs and the big guns. During the day, we worked in the fields or looked for food. At night, we went down to the shelters.

If we heard an aeroplane near the village during the day, everybody had to run down to the shelters. Everyone was frightened of the big bombs. We had to stay in the shelters until the aeroplanes had gone. When it was clear, we had to go back to work.

We couldn't build any fires during the night because if any soldiers saw a fire, they might come to us. It might have been dangerous.

Oh, it was hard for us in the war. Many people died. The fighting took a long time to finish. Some people died from malaria. At the start of the war, some women were pregnant. The war was still not finished by the time they gave birth. Can you imagine how difficult it was to give birth during the war?

Some people were in love and got married during the war. If they really love each other now, then when they argue, they can remind each other about when they were in love during the war.

Before the war, Mae Chan was just a small village, not a town. Chiang Rai was already a town, but I had never been there. I heard about it from the soldiers.

INTERVIEWER: What were the Japanese like? Did they rape the girls?

JA-PU'ER: There were never any rapes near the village. I think no soldier would like to rape a hill girl, ha ha, because hill tribe girls aren't beautiful, they look too dirty. But my father, the headman, he warned the girls to be careful. He had heard that the Japanese soldiers took Thai girls to sleep with them in their rooms. After sleeping with them, the soldiers let them go back home.

The big war was an experience for me. I am still not dead. I would like to know how many other old people are left from the big war. Everyone must be very old now, ha ha.

LISU NEW YEAR - Ali-ya

Ali-ya is 18 years old and single, and lives with her parents, brothers and sisters. She attends a Thai school in Mae Chan five days a week.

INERVIEWER: Are you going to dance today Ali-ya?

ALI-YA: Today is an important day, a big day. Everybody dances in big groups around the pole in the middle of the village. I dance once a year. Do you want to come to my house to see my new Lisu clothes? Today I will wear my Lisu clothes to make my parents happy. When we dance, everybody holds hands. There is nothing wrong with that. When it's New Year, everyone has to be friendly. It's a good time. People have to be good together.

INTERVIEWER: Have you a boyfriend who will also be dancing?

ALI-YA: No, but I have many friends. Thai men, Chinese, Lahu and Lisu, they all quite like me. Many men come to see the girls in our village during New Year. Some of the men are students. Some of them are already married. I pretend to like everyone, but really I don't.

During New Year, people from other villages come to see their families, and come to see all the old people in the village to ask to be forgiven for anything that they've done bad in the year. The family would think they were very bad if they didn't come during New Year.

Parents wouldn't be happy if their children didn't come back. People who don't come back must feel very guilty.

I have an elder sister. When she was younger, she went to a Thai school. She married a Thai soldier. She now lives with her husband's parents. She has to live like a Thai. When it is Lisu and Lahu New Year, and we are eating new rice, my sister and her husband come to celebrate with us. For Lisu people, if you come to eat new rice with your family, then you feel you have done the best thing in the whole year.

BUDDHIST, NOT CHRISTIAN - Nakalae

Nakalae is 15 years old and goes to a Thai school in a nearby Thai village. As with most of the children in Ja-pu'er village, she is a close relative of Ja-pu'er, the old headman.

INTERVIEWER: Is your family Buddhist or Christian?

NAKALAE: Buddhist. In our village most people have been Buddhist for a long time. But there are some Christians who come here, they are Chinese Kuomintang. They try to be friendly with the Buddhist people. They want to make the Buddhists convert to Christianity. But it's difficult.

On Saturday and Sunday the Chinese play with many children in the headman's house. They sing about God, and about how God does things for people, about how he does many good things. They like to talk about angels, about angels that help people. The Christians think the angels are very nice, they think everything the angels do is good. They try to explain about Christianity to the children to try and make the children happy. They sing songs.

Many children like to listen to the Christians in the headman's house. The Christians are clever. Sometimes they stay the night in the headman's house. Maybe our headman works for them. Maybe they use our headman to work for them. I don't like it.

We don't want to change our beliefs. We are from the spirits. We used to believe in the spirits, just like the Buddhists. If anybody changes to being Christian, they should feel guilty.

SCHOOLBOY - Chatchai Bandu

Chatchai is 13 years old and goes to the nearby Thai school. He is clever and very articulate and has plans to go to university.

INTERVIEWER: How do you get to school? Do you walk, or do you go by car?

CHATCHAI: There are no cars. I walk with my friends, fifteen of us from the village. We go early every morning. It is not too far from the village, it's only about three kilometres. It takes about half an hour to walk. We are used to walking, we have walked from when we were babies. I don't care about the distance. My parents taught me to walk when I was one year old.

Sometimes I ask my Thai friends to walk somewhere, but they cannot walk far, they cannot walk in the hills. Sometimes we go camping with the school and the Thais can never walk far. But we can. Walking is easy for Lisu children.

I can walk much further than the teachers. My teacher always has to ask me to stop because he gets tired. Some Thais look almost dead after they have been walking.

INTERVIEWER: Do you like going to school with Thais? What are the Thai students like?

CHATCHAI: Oh, yes, I like going to school. Even if I don't like the Thais, I still have to learn with them, there's nowhere to learn in the village. Some Thais are alright and some are very bad.

For them it is easy to understand what the teachers

say. Thai is their language. Some hill tribe boys are very good students, they are clever but their parents don't have enough money for them to learn. Some aren't clever but they like to learn. We try to learn everything, everything in the school, everything the Thais learn, everything they hear. But sometimes it is difficult to understand the Thai words. Thai students like to make fun of us. They say, "Oh, of course, you are not human, you're an animal". Only words, I don't listen.

We want to learn, we don't want trouble. Every time they say bad things to us, we have to ignore it. But we don't forget. When I've finished studying, I want to do something very clever. I want to get my own back on them. But I know it will take a long time to finish studying. Maybe I am not clever, but I intend finishing my studies at university.

Of course Thai children are clever. They have many different things to see, to learn from. They have many ways to learn. They have television and they often go to the town with their parents. They should be clever.

We are hill children. Every day we waste time walking to and from school. When we get back home after school, there is no time to read books because we have to help the family look after the cows and buffaloes, and we have to help our parents look after our younger brothers and sisters and to get firewood and food for the animals. We have no time. It's a very hard life. There is not enough time to do the homework. We have to take it back to school to do. Sometimes the teachers hit hill tribe children.

INTERVIEWER: Have you ever had any fights with the Thai schoolboys?

CHATCHAI: I've never had a fight. Oh, but if I were a Thai boy, I would fight. I never give trouble to the Thai boys, only they make problems for me. They know they can do anything they like. They could give us a very big problem after school, because on the way back we have to walk through the Thai village. Maybe their parents could wait for us and hit us. It could be dangerous. We have to ignore it every time. If we did anything bad to them after school, then it would be difficult to go back to school the next day.

There are often arguments. Sometimes I complain to my teacher. He says I must ignore it. He says I come to school to learn and shouldn't be interested in fighting. He says if I think too much about problems, my head would be too full and I wouldn't be able to learn and I would be more stupid.

Even our teachers are sometimes bad to us. Sometimes when they give us a lesson, we don't understand something so we ask them, "What is this? What is that?" The Thai students laugh and joke. They make us too embarrassed to ask again. Then the teachers get angry and say bad things to us. Sometimes they say we can't speak Thai because we are hill tribe boys. They often tell us that. Not the women teachers, only the men. But not everyone is like that at school. Some of the teachers are very nice, they are friendly to the students. Sometimes they give us food.

INTERVIEWER: Do you like to play games at school?

CHATCHAI: We don't like to play games at school, we can't play properly. If I try and play games with my Thai friends, then some of their friends always make fun of me. They make me want to stop, I get too embarrassed. We cannot have fun at school.

INTERVIEWER: What about when school is over, do you play with your friends in the village?

CHATCHAI: Yes, sir. We like to play when we have finished doing jobs for the family, especially when there is a moon, so everywhere is light. We like to play war. We like to play dirt-bombing the village. Sometimes we go to the woods and play ghosts with the girls. We frighten them. Sometimes we play building houses. I have to be the father. We play families and collect rice stalks to build huts. When it is full-moon, girls like to play hopscotch. In Lisu we call hopscotch **dom-daeng**. Sometimes on Saturdays and Sundays, we go to the river to practise swimming. If my parents knew, they would hit me. I can't swim. It's dangerous to play in the river. My teacher told me I couldn't be a soldier or a policeman if I can't swim.

We have more fun in the village than at school, but we have to go to school to learn, even though we have problems, we still like to go.

COW GIRL - Nakasae

Nakasae is 14 years old and works for the family by taking the cows out to graze every day. She is very pretty and rather shy. Nakasae's mother is a Lahu Shi woman, and so Nakasae wears Lahu clothes rather than Lisu.

NAKASAE: When I take the cows out, I also take some material, a needle and some cotton with me, so I can make my clothes at the same time as looking after the cows. My parents told me I don't have to go to school. They said there is nothing in school. My mother told me to look after the cows every day for the family. When I get married and have a family, my parents will give me many cows and build me a house. After listening to my parents, I think I don't want to go to school. I don't care what my friends think of me, I am happy to look after the cows. I don't want to be clever. If I were clever, I'd have to work very hard.

A WOMAN'S LIFE - Velawan

Velawan is 26 years old, married to a Thai man and has one daughter. She now lives in her husband's village near Mae Chan. She often returns to her home village to see her family and friends, and on special occasions likes to wear her Lisu clothes.

VELAWAN: My father is Lisu and my mother is Lahu. When my father married my mother he had to live like a Lahu man. He wears Lisu and Lahu clothes. I am a daughter. I married a Thai man and have one daughter. My daughter must be a mixure of Thai, Lisu and Lahu. I want to raise my child as a Thai. I want to teach her to be clever, and to make her go to school early. Thai people have an easy life. When she grows up, I will make her marry a Thai. At the end of my life, there will be no more hill tribe people in my family.

A hill woman has a very difficult life, a very hard life. We never have any freedom. Everything a hill woman does, she does for the family, not for herself. She can never have a good time for herself. It is a bit better for her when she is a baby because her parents have to take care of her, to look after her. But as soon as she can work for her family, she has to.

There is not much work to do for a man. A man likes to be boss. Some men, or boys, go to school, some just hang about. If there is hard work to be done, they let a woman do it. Most people think it is the woman who has to work. I am fed up with doing all the work. I don't want to be inferior to a man. That's why I married a Thai man. We eat well, we live well, we have a good life, a better life than I had before.

INTERVIEWER: What does a hill tribe woman usually do in the morning?

VELAWAN: From the time she gets up, until it's getting dark, she has to do everything. Every day it's the same.

INTERVIEWER: What does she do?

VELAWAN: A Lisu woman, like all women, washes her hands and face as soon as she gets up. Then a Lisu woman has to build the fire, boil the rice, and at the same time as checking the rice and the fire, she has to chop the vegetables for the pigs and sometimes mill the corn and rice for animal feed. As soon as it's light, she gives the feed to the pigs. The pigs eat before the family eat. Then the woman has to cook for the family. After eating breakfast, the woman has to clean the house, sweep the floor and wash the plates. Then she has to go to the fields to work. When she stops for lunch, she has to make her clothes. It's very boring making clothes. Before she returns home, she has to look for vegetables to carry home and cook for the family for dinner. She has to do the same every day. She has to work for years and years.

INTERVIEWER: What time must the woman get up in the morning?

VELAWAN: Now it's not too early, now it's a little bit better. They can get up late now, but late is not after five o'clock. In the past when my mother was younger, when I was a little child, my mother used to get up at three o'clock every morning. She went to bed late and got up early. She had many children.

Now I have got used to getting up at five o'clock. I don't need to get the water from outside the village. In the past, when I lived with my parents, I used to get up at three every morning and go to get the water for everyone in the family to use when they got up. I only had a little time to sleep. Nowadays the women have a better life, they don't have to get the water. Now they have piped water from the mountain.

For women, there is nothing interesting in life. Men are selfish. If I could, I would change men. I'd make them work for the women, I'd let them see how hard life is for the women.

A man has a good time starting from when he first comes out of the womb. The mother, a woman, does everything for him. Especially hill tribe men have a good life. When he gets married, the wife, a woman, has to do everything for him.

A woman cannot look after the money. In everything, she has to ask the man first. But the money is from her work in the fields, from selling vegetables and the crops. The money in the husband's pocket is from selling the woman's sweat. She has to ask if she wants to buy something. She can't buy anything if the man says no. But a man can buy whatever he wants. He can even gamble.

INTERVIEWER: Can the woman complain if the man gambles?

VELAWAN: Um, yes. She can say something, but after she says something, there is a big argument. Nothing good comes of it. Sometimes he hits her. Sometimes he says, if his woman is lazy, he must look for one more wife to help her with her work in the fields.

CHAPTER SIX
KAREN

1) **My Village** - Boon-beng Gangyang, 32.
   The headman of Ban Doi describes his village.
2) **People are Changing** - Jangair, 67.
   An elderly Karen woman complains about changing values in the younger generation.
3) **Dress-Divorce-Death** - Subaen, 56.
   Three aspects of traditional Karen culture outlined.
4) **House Spirit** - Saokam Gangyang, 30.
   Saokam explains why Karen households sometimes hesitate to offer hospitality to strangers.
5) **Tattoos** - Leur Prom-muang, 65.
   Tattoos to win a Karen bride and tattoos for protection against dog bites, knife cuts, stabbing, bullets, scorpions and lightning, Leur has them all.
6) **Going to the Village School** - Somsak, 7.
   Somsak talks about his beautiful Thai teacher and the punishment she gives him for being naughty.
7) **An Old Man and his Two Blind Daughters** - Oo-gao Gangyang, 77.
   Since his wife's death, Oo-gao has had to look after his two blind daughters single-handedly. He tells of the difficulties.
8) **A Strange Village in the Jungle on the Burmese Border** - Jantong Muang-dee, 60.
   Jantong describes a visit he once made to a remote and very strange Karen village on the Burmese border.

MY VILLAGE - Boon-beng Gangyang

Boon-beng is 32 years old and has been the headman of Ban Doi village for five years. He is married and has one daughter. Neither Boon-beng nor his wife intend having any more children, thereby avoiding the financial burden of having a large family. They live an organised and very busy life.

BOON-BENG: Most of the people in the village are Pwo Karen, but they call themselves Yang Daeng (Red Karen). They originate from Lee in Lamphun Province. They left Lee a long time ago, about eighty years ago. The village was founded in the Buddhist year 2458 (Christian year 1915). There were only five families then. The rest of the people came a little later. They had to build the village. I don't know on which day or month they started because there are no documents. The people in the village still argue about it, even now. About moving the village, Karen people nearly always move in big families. Most people in the village are Karen.

The village with its land covers a very big area. One side is very close to Doi Luang mountain. Most of the people in the village are farmers and have paddy fields and animals. But they will do any type of work. The village population is over six hundred. There aren't many children.

Every Karen boy and girl goes to school. In the past the children went to school in a nearby Thai village, but now our village has a school. The parents didn't like their children going too far from home.

Most people speak their own language and also Northern Thai. They are Buddhists, but they still believe in the traditional spirits. Every year they have a ceremony for the Lord of Land and Water. They still believe in spirits, they think spirits can make them lucky and happy.

Every year they used to have a ceremony for the whole village, but now because of the new road being built through the village, and it being difficult to stop people coming into the village during the ceremony, they have to have the ceremony in their houses instead. It lasts for three days and is usually held sometime between January and May.

The village was here even before the nearby Thai villages. Karen people still wear their traditional clothes. In the past they used to be poor, but now the people in the village have a better life.

I am the ninth headman. The first headman, the founder, his name was Meun-phom. He was the most important man in the village eighty years age. Most of the men in the village are grandsons of Meun-phom. Some nephews are still alive, but now they are very old.

PEOPLE ARE CHANGING - Jangair

Jangair is 67 years old and is related to Boon-beng, the headman. Her mother was Thai, but Jangair considers herself to be pure Karen. She is now too old and frail to work in the fields but still makes herself useful by helping to run the household of one of her granddaughters.

JANGAIR: I come from Lee in Lamphun Province. My mother was Thai, she married my father, a Karen man. He came from Burma. He was a mahout, he worked with elephants. His job was to take elephants from the Burmese border to Lee. He met my mother in Lee and they got married and had one child. That was me, I was the child. Then they moved to Ban Doi. We followed the other Karen people who had come before. I grew up in Ban Doi and married a Karen man. My mother was Thai, but after she married she had to change her life and become a Karen woman.

INTERVIEWER: Did your mother have to change her name?

JANGAIR: No, she didn't have to change her name, but she had to be a Karen wife. I am my father's daughter, so I had to be a Karen daughter. I had a normal Karen life. We always wore Karen clothes and we believed in Karen spirits and culture. My father was a Karen man, he used to be a famous elephant handler. He was a very good mahout. In the past, Karen families, every family, had elephants. Sometimes when Karen couples got married, the dowry was paid in elephants.

INTERVIEWER: How many children have you?

JANGAIR: I had nine children. One was stillborn and two died after birth, after only two days. The other six are all still alive. They are all married and have children. Some of their children go to school in the town. Some of them don't like it that their parents still keep the Karen culture.

INTERVIEWER: What do you think about today's children? Is it a good idea to let the children go to school in the town?

JANGAIR: Oh, I don't like it at all. The children have their heads full of modern ideas. When they come back home, they bring friends with them, Thai friends, and they don't like to wear Karen clothes. It's good to study, but I see that every child who has an education is different, they change their ideas about things. I don't like it.

The children don't like me, or their parents, to believe in spirits, or to follow traditional Karen culture. Always when they come back home they like to talk about modern things, things like fashion. They like to talk about what a good time they've had at school. Sometimes I have heard them talking together about nice clothes, modern clothes. No, I don't like it.

Karen children in the past never wore Thai clothes. If somebody wore Thai clothes, it was considered very bad. If a girl wore trousers, then things were made difficult for her. People would joke about her. Now the children have changed a lot. Some of them have been wearing Thai clothes now for two or three years. Now they don't like to weave cloth at home, now they prefer to buy it. But I suppose it's not all bad, they still wear their traditional clothes when they want to go somewhere.

Now the children are not shy. They do whatever they want to, they don't ask their parents first. Now they are modern children. Now they are bad. They like to fight with other people. They drink whisky. They make little problems become big problems and they get angry easily. They become just like Thais.

The old people of the past, people of my age, and my sons' and daughters' age, when they had an argument with friends, there was no real problem. They just said sorry to their friends and then forgot all about it. They didn't like to fight, or even kill people over nothing. When we had a celebration we used to drink whisky and visit other villages, many other villages. We would always be many people, but we never had any trouble. If somebody did something wrong, they apologised. They still listened to the old people.

But now the children have very bad hearts. When the children have a party or celebration, and someone accidentally treads on someone's toes, they hit and kill that person. A big group of them fight. Oh, they are bad people, really no good. The children now are very bad, worse than before. Now, when there is a fair in a Thai village near here, there are always a lot of Thai girls dancing, and there are many people from other places. And the Karen children have to go. Oh, such a headache.

I am frightened of the children. They are very lazy. In the past, when I was young, when I was a girl, we helped each other harvest the rice. Girls and boys sang

Karen songs together. We had a lot of fun. At night, girls and boys used to help thresh the rice, they would help everyone until it was all finished. Then when we had finished, we had a big celebration for the new rice. We never had problems about girls being raped, or girls getting pregnant before marriage. Everyone was polite to each other. Oh, it was so different from what it's like now. Karen girls were very strict, boys could not touch them. It is different now.

DRESS - DIVORCE - DEATH - Subaen

Subaen is 56 years old and lives in a large new house with her husband, widowed son and two grandchildren. Having suffered three deaths in her immediate family in recent years and a fire which totally destroyed her home, Subaen is all the more careful to avoid displeasing the spirits, and at all times adheres faithfully to the traditions of her people.

INTERVIEWER: Subaen, when Karen women are single they wear a simple white dress. Is it possible for a married woman to sometimes wear a single woman's dress just for a change?

SUBAEN: Oh, they cannot, they cannot, the house spirit wouldn't like it, and it's against the ancestor spirits. The women wouldn't like to try because the 'grandmother-ancestor-spirit' says they shouldn't. She says if a married woman went back to wearing white again, a tiger would come to eat her. Once there was jungle, very dense jungle, around the village and there were many wild animals, including tigers. In the past somebody in the village saw a tiger nearby. I think if a married woman were to wear white clothes again, the tiger would come to eat her.

INTERVIEWER: Can Karen couples get divorced when they have problems with their marrige?

SUBAEN: Oh, they cannot do that. If they got married in the first place and have lived together, then surely they have to love each other. In traditional Karen culture there is no divorce or separation. Even if they are very bad to each other, they still have to live together, even if there is a big argument. If they were to divorce, the people in the village would think that they were very bad people. Nobody would want to be friendly with such people. No, they cannot divorce.

INTERVIEWER: Do the Karen bury or cremate their dead?

SUBAEN: It is Karen tradition to bury people when they die. But before they are buried, many women sing songs while walking around the dead body. They sing all day and night. Sometimes they keep the body for two days, it depends on the family of the dead person.

INTERVIEWER: What do the women sing about?

SUBAEN: They sing about the dead person, about the person's life, about what she did, about how nice she was and about the good things she has done. And they sing about the good things to come for her now that she is dead. They sing:
Now you are dead, off you go,
Don't worry about us,
Go well, eat well, live well,
Eat only very good food,
Don't worry about your children,
We will help you.
They have to tell the dead person which way to go to get to heaven. Sometimes they sing for two or three days. Everyone in the family of the dead person has

to stop work, all work. They have to stop spinning and weaving, and stop eating certain vegetables. Usually they stop for three days, but some families stop for as long as a month.

HOUSE SPIRIT - Saokam Gangyang

Saokam is 30 years old and is married to Boonbeng, the headman (see My Village). She works in the fields, looks after the house and helps to entertain guests, many of whom are Thai local government officials.

INTERVIEWER: Is it difficult being the headman's wife?

SAOKAM: Normally it's not too difficult. There are no real problems, unless we have guests in the house. Usually I don't need to help my husband in his official capacity. My husband and I still work in the fields like everyone else in the village. The only problem I have is when we have guests staying. Sometimes we have Thai guests, they don't know about Karen culture. In our village, in our houses, we still believe in the traditional culture, we still believe in the house spirit. We haven't forgotten our culture, even though we are a modern village and have trucks coming through every day now.

Every time we have a man and woman, a couple, staying in our house, I have to tell them they must have separate bedrooms. The woman must sleep in the small bedroom, and the man in the living room. I have to make up the beds every time. Sometimes to be polite, my husband moves his bedding out of our room and goes to sleep in the living room with the guest.

INTERVIEWER: Does this custom apply only to Thais?

SAOKAM: No, no. The son and daughter-in-law can sleep together, but all other men and women, Thai or Karen, have to have separate rooms. It is because of the house spirit. Every time people come to stay, I have to explain this to them. The lowland people don't know about our culture, especially townspeople.

In Karen culture if you knock against the walls, floor or supports of a house, the house spirit doesn't like it and we have to buy a pig to make an offering to the spirit. Sometimes people from the district office or the malaria office come here to work. Sometimes they hit the floor or the walls of the house by mistake. Then they have to pay two baht to us so we can go and buy a pig for the spirit. Sometimes they know about the spirit but can't help hitting the wall. Or sometimes the electricity workers come to the house and knock on the walls. They must also pay two baht. Two baht to buy a pig for the house spirit. We can only ask for two baht from the person who knocks against the house. Two baht to buy a pig, of course it's never enough. Even a small pig now costs two or three hundred baht. But we have believed in spirits for a long time, for hundreds and hundreds of years. We can't change it now.

Sometimes when people stay in our house they buy food to cook, sometimes they buy pork from the market. If they bring pork to our house, it's contrary to the wishes of the house spirit and they have to pay two baht. Any pork, or even pig fat, that is not from our house or farm cannot be brought into our house.

In the past, lowland Thais used to sell pigs from door to door. They didn't know our culture. They used to carry the pigs in big baskets on the backs of their motorbikes and come to the village to try and sell them. Every time that they brought a pig inside our fence, it was against the house spirit. Even live pigs cannot be brought to our houses.

Sometimes during the day we go away from our house. We shut the door but often do not lock it. Sometimes the electricity people come to fix something in the house, or they come to read the meter. Sometimes they knock on the wall or floor, but we don't know. Then after two or three days someone in the family gets ill for no apparent reason. So we have to ask the soothsayer for the reason. The soothsayer looks into the past. He says someone came to the house and knocked against it and thus disturbed the house spirit. So then we have to go and look for whoever it was who went into the house, and ask for the two baht so we can buy a pig. Often people offer more than two baht, but we can't take it, we can't take more than the two baht.

This is the main reason why Karen people sometimes hesitate about offering to let people stay in their houses. They don't like to have to fork out a few hundred baht for a pig all the time.

Another thing about pigs, if we have a sow that gives birth to only female piglets, we cannot keep the pig, we have to kill it for the spirit. We can't sell it, but we can eat it. Also a dog has to be killed if it has only female puppies. We have to kill it to placate the house spirit. And if a chicken makes a noise like a cock in the morning, it, too, has to be killed. It's very unusual for a chicken to make a noise like a cock. Isn't that right?

INTERVIEWER: Yes, of course, chickens don't normally make a noise like a cock.

SAOKAM: Any chicken that makes a noise like a cock has to be killed. We have to sacrifice it to the house spirit. The house spirit is very important in our lives.

TATTOOS - Leur Prom-muang

Leur is 65 years old and is a former headman of Ban Doi. He lives with his wife in a large and very impressive-looking house - a house which has fifty-six treetrunk-size supporting posts - and spends his days taking care of his farm, visting his many friends and relatives in the village and smoking his favourite home-made pipe

INTERVIEWER: Your name is Prom-muang, are you related to Meun-phom, the founder of the village?

LEUR: Yes, my father was one of Meun-phom's sons. My family name is Prom-muang. My father took the name from my grandfather's name.

INTERVIEWER : On your arms, your back, everywhere you have tattoos. Can you tell me about them?

LEUR : Oh, I don't know where to start talking. If Karen men don't have any tattoos, then it's the same as if they were a woman. If they consider themselves to be men, then they must have tattoos. Every Karen man has to have tattoos to show his character. The women like a man to have tattoos. The women are not interested in a man without them. Even if he is smart, or clever, or good-looking, without them the women are not interested. They think a man who doesn't have tattoos is feeble like a woman.

But it is not only the men that have tattoos, some wilful Karen women have them as well. Only a few women have them, around their lower calves.

INTERVIEWER: Can anybody make the tattoos, or do you have a special person to do it? Or do the spirits do them through a medium?

LEUR: Yes, we have a specialist who does them but it's nothing to do with spirits. Anybody can learn how to do tattoos. To have tattoos made shows a man is confident with the women. Do you know I had tattoos like these made (displaying his arms), this is why my wife likes me.

INTERVIEWER: Is that true?

LEUR'S WIFE: Oh yes, of course. If he hadn't had good tattoos, I would not have married him.

LEUR: She was the prettiest women in the village. Many men wanted to marry her. All of her suitors had tattoos, every single one of them. But I had the best. She liked mine the best.

INTERVIEWER: When did you have them done?

LEUR: Oh, when I was young, when I was not quite twenty years old. I had seen my brother's tattoos when I was younger. He could really show off to the girls. I thought of myself as a man, so I had to have tattoos for the girls as well.

I had them done. They took a long time to finish. Oh, it hurt a lot, especially from my waist to my thighs, where I had them made to look like a pair of shorts. I knew it would hurt a lot, but I was doing it for a girl, for my love. I had a lot of patience. I had them everywhere on my body, except on the palms of my hands and under my feet.

INTERVIEWER: Is there any significance to the many different designs on your arms?

LEUR: Some of the designs are for protection from dog bites, some are for protection against knife cuts and stabbing, some for protection against bullets and some for scorpions, many different things, oh, and some for lightning.

INTERVIEWER: Is the writing on the tattoos Karen or Pali? I know it's not Thai or Burmese.

LEUR: The writing is Karen, in Karen script.

INTERVIEWER: Do your sons have tattoos like yours?

LEUR: Some of my sons have them all over their bodies, but some have them only on their arms. Every son has tattoos for protection against dog bites. I would have liked all of my sons to have been covered in tattoos, it looks so beautiful. They would have looked so impressive when they took off their shirts. But they haven't enough patience.

Some of my sons work in the south, they work as car mechanics. Some are married and living in the village.

GOING TO THE VILLAGE SCHOOL - Somsak

Somsak is 7 years old and goes to the village school five days a week. His mother died when he was two and he now lives with his father and his grandmother. His father is a soldier and is often away from home. Somsak's favourite hobby is drawing pictures, especially pictures of aeroplanes and helicopters.

INTERVIEWER: Hello Somsak. I see you are in school uniform. Where do you go to school?

SOMSAK: Hello miss. My school is in the village.

INTERVIEWER: Do you like school?

SOMSAK: Yes, miss.

INTERVIEWER: Can you read and write Thai yet?

SOMSAK : Yes miss, now I can write my father's name, my grandfather's and grandmother's name and many other words. My teacher she is nice, her name is Pan-ngam. Her name means beautiful.

INTERVIEWER: Is she beautiful?

SOMSAK: She is really beautiful, but she is a very strict teacher. When I am in my classroom, I like to play with my friends. I like to speak in Karen with my friends. If my teacher knew, she might hit me.

INTERVIEWER: What does she teach you?

SOMSAK: Everything. She teaches everyone to speak Thai. Sometimes I say something in Karen in the classroom, and she tells me and my friends that if anyone speaks Karen in the classroom, we have to pay two baht for the teacher spirit. But she never gets two baht. There is no teacher spirit.

INTERVIEWER: Do you have lunch at school?

SOMSAK: Yes, miss.

INTERVIEWER: Every day?

SOMSAK:
No. At my school we have free lunch on two days, on Monday and Tuesday. My teacher cooks it, it's really delicious.

INTERVIEWER : So usually you take lunch with you?

SOMSAK: Yes, miss. I have to take lunch three times a week, miss.

INTERVIEWER: Do you have many friends at school.

SOMSAK: I have eighteen friends, seven boys and eleven girls. I love all my friends. My teacher loves me very much. Sometimes when I do something wrong, if my friends are not there, she doesn't hit me. She loves me.

But at school I don't like having to clean the classroom. Every morning we have to do it. If we don't do it, our teacher hits us. But if I don't do it, my teacher tells me to clean the toilet.

INTERVIEWER: Oh, do you have to do it?

SOMSAK: Yes, miss, I have to do it. It's very dirty work, worse than cleaning the classroom. I often get cross when I have to do it. Sometimes I have arguments with my teacher, but only inside my head, I can't really argue with her.

AN OLD MAN AND HIS TWO BLIND DAUGHTERS - Oo-gao

> *Oo-gao is 77 and was born in Burma. In his younger days he was an elephant trainer in the Burmese jungles. His wife of many years died two years ago. Of their ten children, six have already died. Of the remaining four, one, a daughter, has moved away from Ban Doi and one, a son, has married and lives nearby. The other two, both daughters, are blind and disabled and remain at home under Oo-gao's constant care. He himself is now in poor health and worries greatly about their future after his death.*

OO-GAO: My wife died two years ago. Since I lost my wife, I've had a very hard time. I've had to look after my two big daughters, both of whom are nearly blind. I am old, now I am seventy-seven years old. Do you see, I am seventy-seven and I still have to look after my blind children. They are both quite old, one is fifty-two and the other is forty-nine. Neither of them is quite right in the head. And we are poor and I have to do the cooking.

INTERVIEWER: Where do you get the money to live from?

OO-GAO: I cannot make any money by working but we have a few paddy fields which we rent out to someone else. We share the rice they produce. Some of the rice we keep to eat and some we sell. That's all we have. There's nothing else. The money we get from the rice has to last all year. Sometimes when we are lucky, we can make twenty thousand baht from the rice. We keep some of the money for buying medicine and we use some for making clothes for my daughters. They have two dresses each. After that, there's never much left. In the past, when my wife was still alive, she made clothes for my daughters and for me. Now I have to pay someone to make them.

Sometimes we like to eat meat or fish so we keep some of the rice money to buy meat or fish. But we don't buy it often. Usually we eat only vegetables. We don't buy the vegetables, we find them on my land. If we do buy any, we buy very cheap ones with no taste. We have to eat. We never have good food. Neither of my daughters can cook because they can't see properly, and one has a bad leg and a bad hand.

INTERVIEWER: How many people are there in your family?

OO-GAO: I had many children, six are dead and four are still alive. Now I have three daughters left and one son. The last one, the youngest one, she married and lives somewhere else. She has children. And my son married. He has his home in the village here. He lives near to my house. Oh, you know, sometimes my son brings his children to me to look after. I cannot refuse. My daughters and I have to look after my son's children. One of my daughters has bad eyes, ears and a leg, and I am a little bit unwell now as well, but we have to look after my grandchildren. If I complain to my son, he thinks I am very bad. He's considered rich for this village. He gives me food when I look after his children. If I don't look after them, he doesn't bring me any food.

INTERVIEWER: It must be difficult for you to do everything for your daughters.

OO-GAO: It is difficult. It's difficult for me to cook for them and difficult to look for food for us all. I can't teach them to do anything, they never seem to learn. Both of them are quite old now. Sometimes they help me a little with the cooking, but they don't do anything else.

They cannot walk far - they don't know where to go. They never leave the garden. They haven't been anywhere in forty or fifty years. They are frightened of cars and of strangers.

I am not sure what to do. If I die before them, it will be very difficult for them. I worry very much about them. I need someone to look after them. I would give my land, my farm and my house to anybody who would look after them.

INTERVIEWER: Do your daughters get bored sitting at home all the time?

OO-GAO: One of them does. She used to say she would like to go somewhere. Once she tried to go somewhere on her own. She went for two or three hours. I waited for her to return until late afternoon, but she still hadn't come back. I didn't know where she had gone. I went to look for her. I found her sitting in a hut near the end of the village. She had got lost and was waiting for someone to walk past so she could ask them to take her home. After that, she never wanted to go anywhere again. Sometimes she says it would be better to let her die.

INTERVIEWER: What happened to her leg, her hand, her eyes and ears?

OO-GAO: When she was young, she had a very bad fever. She had a very high temperature and was unconscious for two days. When she came to, I treated her with herbal medicine. There was no doctor and it was too far to the hospital. Later on, I noticed it was difficult for her to move her arms and legs. I didn't know what to do. It was just a fever, not a bad wound or anything. After many months, after she had grown a bit, I realised that her arm, leg, hand and ears were very weak. And they never got stronger.

INTERVIEWER: Do you sometimes get fed up with your daughters? Do you ever have arguments with them?

OO-GAO: Oh, I do get fed up with them sometimes. I can never go anywhere. I have such a boring life. I can't even go to the fields. But arguments? No, we never have arguments.

I have been ill now for five years. There isn't much blood in my head. The doctor told me that half my body is paralysed. One whole side of my body has no feeling.

I don't know why but I am often upset. My friends have children to look after them now that they are old, but for me, I am old, and I am a father, but I have to look after my children, my daughters. Nobody looks after me.

A STRANGE VILLAGE IN THE JUNGLE ON THE BURMESE BORDER - Jantong Muang-dee

Jantong is 60 years old and lives in a Karen village near Ban Doi. He once lived in Ban Doi and is a close relative of Subaen (see Dress-Divorce-Death).

JANTONG: Once, in the past, I walked to the Burmese border. I went to a very old Karen village. The people there lived in small groups. They still believed in the religion of the Brahmins. They were so strict. Everybody in the village had to do what they were told. The village was very private, there was something very strange about it. Nobody could enter the village area without first giving a very good reason why they wanted to go there. Even other Karen had to have a good reason.

There was one house that was looked after by an old woman. If anybody went to the village, they had to stay in that house. I had to ask the old woman to let me stay.

I was very frightened of the Karen men in the village. They looked so unfriendly. I saw them training to fight with sticks and knives. I couldn't walk wherever I wanted.

The first night I stayed there, I didn't feel safe. The village was very strange, very quiet. Everybody in the village was proud, they didn't like the goverment or anyone to interfere with them.

INTERVIEWER: How different was their religion to Buddhism?

JANTONG: Er, the Brahmin monk is similar to the Thai Buddhist monk, except the Brahmin monks have very long hair. I don't know much about their religion but I saw that no woman had a husband. Some of the monks looked young.

I went to see two monks. They lived in a cave and looked after two elephant tusks. The tusks were very beautiful. I asked them for how long they had had the tusks. I was very surprised when they answered that many ancestors had died since they first got them. They said they were over a thousand years old. They were very important tusks. The monks in the past had carved pictures onto them. They were very beautiful and very important for the village. They kept the tusks in the cave to keep them safe. The two monks told me that on special religious days, they take the tusks outside to do something with them. They told me that women were not allowed to touch the tusks.

The first day I stayed there, everyone was very unfriendly to me. I didn't like it. But after one night I felt better.

INTERVIEWER: Did they have a school in the village? Or anything else?

JANTONG: They had nothing from the government. There was no school and no hospital, no cars or motorbikes, and not even a bicycle. They didn't like anything new in the village. The village didn't like to have anything to do with the government. If anybody from the government told them to do something, they killed them. Even other Karen people from nearby villages couldn't tell them anything.

They had one Brahmin monk who was like a headman. I don't know what they ate. I'm not sure if they ate meat or not, but I saw some dried meat hanging outside a house. The meat was from a wild animal. I saw a tiger skin. Around the village there was jungle, very thick jungle.

The people there spoke North Karen. I saw them writing in Karen. I can read some Karen. When I was young I went to study Karen writing, but after I came to Thailand I didn't use Karen writing again. Not many people can read Karen. Now I've forgotten. Many of the people in the village could also speak Burmese.

I only went there once, I never went there again.

EIGHT VILLAGES

We visited and interviewed people from eight villages in Chiang Rai Province. These villages, with brief details, are as follows:

1) **Lao Shi Guai village,** Mae Chan District. A small Yao village of less than fifteen households situated in a valley at the foot of a range of forested hills west of Mae Chan. All but one of the Yao interviews were from this village.

2) **Ba Rai Luang village,** Mae Chan District. A large, prosperous, Yao village in the lower foothills of Doi Luang mountain east of Chiangsaen.

3) **Paca Sook Jai village,** Mae Chan District. A large traditional Loimi-Akha village of over seventy households situated high up in the mountains approximately six kilometres from Mae Salong.

4) **Mai Paca village,** Mae Chan District. A small and very traditional U Lo-Akha village in the mountains near Mae Salong.

5) **Kiew Khan village** (Lahu section), Chiangkhong District. A small, poor, Lahu Shi village of post-1975 refugees from Laos, situated above the large Hmong village of Kiew Khan.

6) **Kiew Khan village,** Chiangkhong District. A large White Hmong village of nearly one hundred households situated in mountains overlooking Laos and the Mekong river northwest of Chiangkhong. Kiew Khan is located in one of the few remaining areas of primary forest left in northern Thailand.

7) **Ja-pu'er village,** Mae Chan District. A large, fairly prosperous, Lisu-Lahu Shi village lying at the foot of a range of low forested hills west of Mae Chan. Nearly every family in the village is of mixed Lisu-Lahu descent.

8) **Ban Doi village,** Mae Chan District. A large well established lowland Pwo Karen village lying on the Mae Bong river east of Mae Chan and south of Chiangsaen.

MAP 3 AREA LOCATION MAP

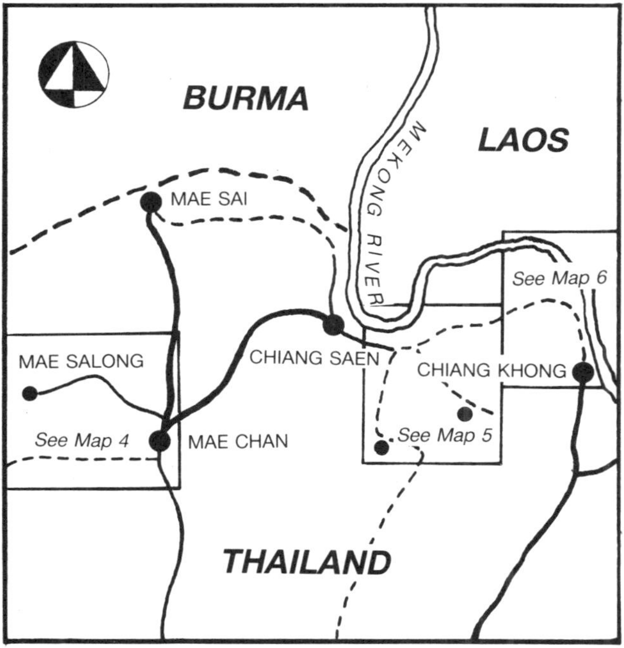

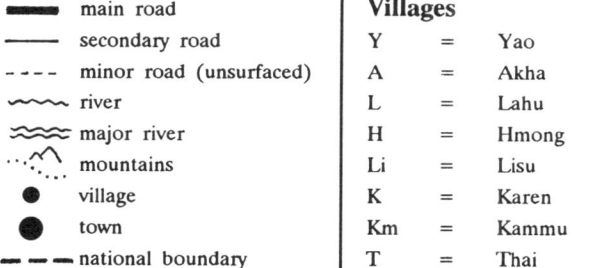

Legend

▬▬▬	main road
───	secondary road
----	minor road (unsurfaced)
∼∼∼	river
≋≋≋	major river
⋯⩙⋯	mountains
●	village
⬤	town
▬ ▬ ▬	national boundary

Villages

Y	=	Yao
A	=	Akha
L	=	Lahu
H	=	Hmong
Li	=	Lisu
K	=	Karen
Km	=	Kammu
T	=	Thai

MAP 4 MAE CHAN - MAE SALONG AREA

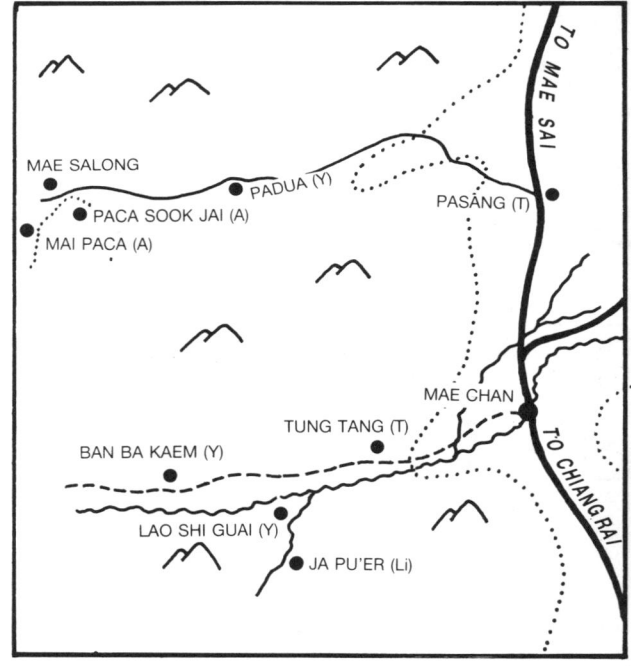

MAP 5 BAN DOI - BA RAI LUANG AREA

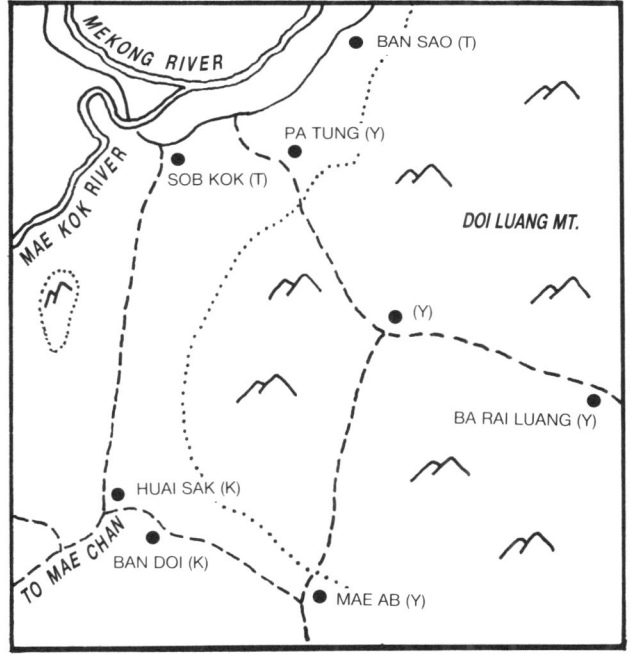

MAP 6 CHIANGKHONG AREA

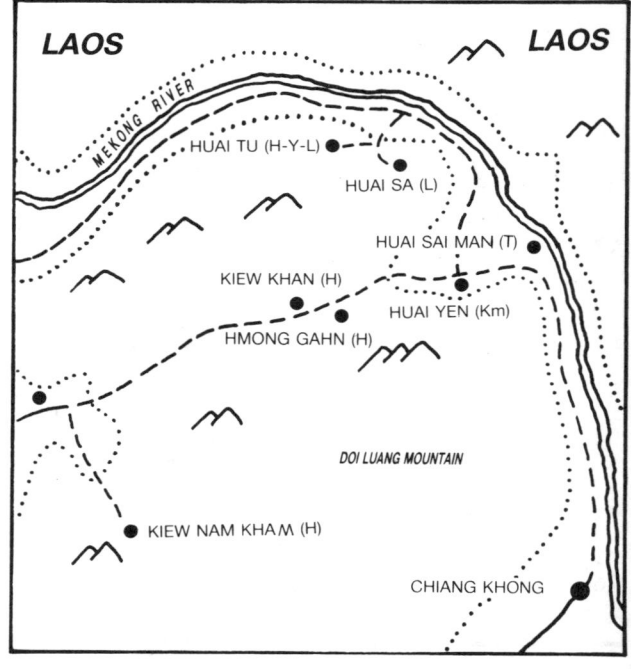

RECOMMENDATIONS FOR VISITORS

There follow a few recommended places to stay for anybody who wants to visit the northern part of Chiang Rai Province, in particular for those people who want to call in on any of the eight villages of this book. The recommendations are based solely on the authors' personal experience.

The four most convenient centres in the area for those people who want to see the hilltribes are Chiang Rai, Mae Chan, Mae Salong and Chiang Khong. Chiang Saen and Mae Sai, although of interest in themselves, are not well located for trips into the hills.

CHIANG RAI is the principal town in the region and was founded in 1262 by King Mengrai. A bronze statue of the king can be seen in the town. Chiang Rai is growing fast and the central streets are often clogged with traffic. The advertisers' claims of it's quiet, peaceful, almost rural atmosphere should not be believed. This may have been true ten years ago, even five years ago perhaps, but this is certainly not the case now. Still despite the noise and bustle, Chiang Rai is a friendly, distinctively northern town, which, being equally well located for organised tours into the hills as for individual trips by motorbike and car, attracts a steady stream of tourists and travellers to its many hotels and guesthouses. Standards of accommodation in Chiang Rai are consistently high.

MAE CHAN is a bustling market town that attracts many Akha, Lisu, Yao and Lahu people to it's central market-but accomodation here is limited. The best place to stay is the highly recommended "Laan Tong Lodge" directly west of the town - follow the signposts. From Laan Tong Lodge you can easily walk to Lao Shi Guai (Yao) and Ban Ja-pu'er (Lisu) as well as to many other hill tribe villages.

MAE SALONG is a Chinese settlement situated in beautiful surroundings high up in the mountains west of Mae Chan. Since 1962 Mae Salong has been home to former soldiers of the Chinese Kuomintang army- Nationalists from per-1949 China. The town has a distinct Chinese flavour about it, and to many conjures up the very picture of a small town in China's Yunnan Province. Many Akha and Lisu, as well as Shan people come to the town to sell market produce and to purchase consumer products; fabrics, sewing needles, nails, torch batteries and such like. There are three guesthouses, all of which are pleasant places in which to stay, and all of which can point you in the right direction for walks to Akha, Lisu and Shan villages. The two Akha villages, Paca Sook Jai and Mai Paca are easily reached from the town. On the summit of the hill overlooking the town there is a modern Chinese-style resort complex. This resort caters mainly to ethnic Chinese tourists from Bangkok.

CHIANG KHONG lies on the banks of the Mekong river and is another lively market town that attracts hill tribe peoples in large numbers, particularly Hmong, but also Yao, and Lahu, as well as people belonging to two tribal groups not so well know in Thailand, the Khamu and Lawa. Chiang Khong is a friendly little town with a pleasant atmosphere. There are two Chinese hotels and one guesthouse along the main street. The guesthouse - Tam-mi-la - is a comfortable place to stay and the owners can supply you with maps and information on the local area. There is also a resort complex a little way outside the town.

From Chiang Khong it is easy to find lifts in Hmong-owned pick-up trucks that can drop you in, or near to, a number of hill tribe villages, including the Hmong-Lahu village of Kiew Khan. In Kiew Khan itself there is a small friendly guesthouse situated in pleasant surroundings.

The two other villages, Ban Doi (Karen) and Ba Rai Luang (Yao) are best reached from Chiang Saen, although Ban Doi can also be reached fairly easily from Mae Chan. Unlike the other six villages featured in this book, Ban Doi and Ban Rai Luang are not located in particularly scenic locations.

VISITING HILL TRIBE VILLAGES

Whether alone or on an organised tour a little personal contact in a hill tribe village goes a long way. There are, however, some things which the visitor may be unaware of, and which should be avoided in order to minimize disturbance.

GENERAL CONSIDERATIONS

1) Do not enter a house displaying a toboo sign by the door. These signs are star-shaped flimsey bamboo devices and are usually placed just above the door. Another warning sign is a branch stuck into the lower part of the roof near the door. The presence of such indicators normally means there is a special spirit ritual in progress inside the house, normally one which only family members may attend.

2) Generally it is best not to enter a house unless invited to do so. This is a matter of common courtesy. Once inside the house visitors should be particularly wary of touching the spirit altar or cooking stove, as for many of the tribes these objects have special relevance to their animistic beliefs.

3) Do not take photographs of a sick person. Many tribal people believe this may frighten away an already wavering soul or spirit. Be particularly careful when photographing a mother carrying a baby. If the mother obviously wishes that no picture be taken, then desist, as it may be that the child is sick.

4) As visitors and guests you should take extra care not to offend the people of the local culture. Open

displays of affection between couples, kissing in public, taking a shower topless (in the case of women) and making love whilst a guest in a house are all considered 'bad form' and are likely to cause embarrassment.

SPECIFIC DON'TS

We also list a number of considerations relevant to the individual tribes. Many of these points are connected with their animistic beliefs.

YAO - It is forbidden for anyone in a Yao house to put their feet against the household stoves (there are two of them) or to sit nearby and lean back on them.

It is also important not to enter the bedroom of a pregnant woman as the souls of an unborn child are believed easily to be frightened away. Other precautions taken to avoid deformity and miscarriage include care being taken not to spill water on the fireplace, and the avoidance of striking the door or the rice pounder with a knife of any kind. Visitors should always ask permission before taking photographs of children, for the Yao belive if children are startled their souls may be frightened away.

AKHA - An outsider should not walk through an Akha village without entering at least one house and accepting something to eat and drink. There are two doors to an Akha house, it is important for a guest to enter and leave by the same door. Male guests should not enter the women's section of the house, although women guests are free to enter both the men's and the women's sections. The spirit gates located on the main paths leading into the village should on no account be touched.

In fact, if one does not intend entering the village, and therefore entering at least one house, one should not even walk through the gates, and should detour around the village.

LAHU - Visitors should not touch the sacred posts around a Lahu Nyi temple. Some Lahu believe the smell of soap may cause some women's milk to dry up.

HMONG - Visitors to a Hmong village should not enter a Hmong house if a woman inside is near to childbirth. In general it is courteous not to enter a Hmong house until invited to do so by the oldest male member present. This rule does not apply when there are no male family members present.

LISU - Guests to a Lisu house should not enter the bedrooms, should not disturb the ancestor altar and should not sleep with their heads towards the fire. The fireplace is sacred to the Lisu. Visitors should also not stand in the doorway with their feet either side of it. In a Lisu village females should not enter the compound of the village guardian spirit shrine. This roofed shrine is usually located underneath a leafy tree in a fenced area just above the village.

KAREN - Guests to Karen houses are usually directed to sleep on the veranda of the house. This is because the Karen have to avoid a situation where spirits associated with individuals may be in conflict. This veranda-rule also applies to certain family members of the household. Unmarried sons past the age of puberty cannot sleep in the same house with their sisters of marriageable age, they have to sleep on the veranda of a friend's house. Guests should realise that Karen sexual morals are very strict, and any "uncalled-for" sexual behaviour is likely to be frowned upon. In the rice fields it is taboo to hack at, or in any way disturb, any half-burned tree-stumps until after the harvest, as it is thought a spirit referred to as the Crop Grandmother sits on them watching while the rice grows.

DO'S

The big 'Do' in a hill tribe village is to be entertaining. Talk with as many people as you can, no matter how difficult the language barrier. Try out as many words from the word lists as possible, even learn some new ones. Play with the children, admire a girl's good looks, comment on a woman's embroidery. Offer cigarettes to the men in a household and show village people photographs from your home country, even pictures from your travels.

Despite the list of 'don'ts', hill tribe people generally make allowances for people from an alien culture. They themselves are used to meeting and dealing with people from a whole host of cultural backgrounds. Thus, once aware of a few important taboos, the average visitor to a tribal village does not need to worry overly about making any great social-cultural blunders.

USEFUL PHRASES

Most hill tribe people are generally very hospitable to strangers and they enjoy the interest shown by outsiders in their culture and way of life. But few visitors can speak Thai, let alone the individual tribal languages, and even fewer hill tribe people speak English or any other western language, and thus communication can often be difficult. Difficult, yes, but not impossible. Sign language goes surprisingly far in tribal villages, and with the knowledge of just a handfull of words in the native language it is possible to get by fairly easily.

As an aid to communication we list a few useful words and phrases in the individual tribal languages. We also include a Thai word list as many tribal people, particularly the men, speak Thai with little difficulty.

YAO

English	Yao	Thai
where are you going?	ming hai	pai nai
where are you coming from?	ming hai da	pai nai ma
what is your name?	may-eh boa he-ow han yung	chua arai
my name is...	ye-ar bor...	chan chua...
I	ye-ar	chan
you	mo-ay	khun
I don't understand	yem hew	chan mai koujai
yes	tzey	krap (kaa for women)
no	um tzey	mai
thank you	len tzing	kopkhun
what	han-yoon	arai
when	han-jahng	mua-rai

English	Yao	Thai
where	yam-hai	tee-nai
why	zhou-hor	tam-mai
how far	ming go	gee kilo
how much	mer-tsia	tow-rai
to do	zhou	tam
to go	ming	pai
to walk	jang jow	dern
to eat	nee-en hang	kin
house	be-ow	ban
village	lang	moo ban
field	ling	na,rai
water	wum	nam
rice	hang	kou
tea	tsar	nam cha

friend	doy	puen
good	long	dee
never mind / it's nothing	mo ben kou	mai benrai
1	yet	nung
2	ee	sorng
3	poor	sarm
4	pay	see
5	pyar	hah
6	jew	hok
7	seer	jet
8	hyet	paet
9	doer	kou
10	tsee-up	sip
11	tsee-up yet	sip-et
12	tsee-up-njay	sip-sorng

English	Yao	Thai
13	tsee-up-farm	sip-sarm
14	tsee-up-fay	sip-see
15	tsee-up-hum	sip-hah
16	tsee-up-lower	sip-hok
17	tsee-up-see-yet	sip-jet
18	tsee-up-bet	sip-paet
19	tsee-up-chewer	sip-kou
20	nee-tsee-up	yee-sip
100	yet pe	nung roy
1000	yet sin	nung pan

AKHA

English	Akha	Thai
hello	ga-la had-you dumnya	sawadee
goodbye	oh eema day	laa kon, pai la
where are you going?	ee-kerng	pai nai
what is your name?	chum ya-ah you con-tee	chua arai
I	nga	chan
you	ngo	khun
yes	uhh	krap (kaa for women)
no	man-ger	mai
please	gal-a-gum-nya	chern
thank you	goo lon who-lay-marr	kopkhun
what	ad-jay ah	arai
village	pooh	moo ban

English	Akha	Thai
house	yeum	ban
field	ye-yeh haw	na, rai
water	ee-jew	nam
rice	ho	kou
never mind / it's nothing	jie mang-na	mai benrai
1	tdee	nung
2	nee	sorng
3	show	sarm
4	yuk	see
5	nga	hah
6	guo	hok
7	see	jet
8	ye-ar	paet

9	kou
10	sip
11	sip-et
20	yee-sip
100	nung roy
1000	nung pan

	whirr
	tche
	tche-tdee
	nee-che
	tdee-are
	tdee-par

LAHU SHI

English	Lahu Shi	Thai
where are you going?	kao gai-li	pai nai
where are you coming from?	kao gai gaw-la-yi	pai nai ma
what is your name?	nore oh-meh-a-ma-ley	chua arai
my name is...	om-meh...	chan chua...
I	nga	chan

SOME USEFUL PHRASES

English	Lahu Shi	Thai
you	nor	khun
we	ongna	rou
yes	heyo	krap (kaa for women)
no	ma heyo	mai
please	lor	chern
thank you	abu-hi-ya	kopkhun
what	a-toh-lee	arai
when	kah-tah-lee	muarai
where	kao-lee	tee-nai
how much	koi-ma-lee	tow-rai
to go	gai	pai
to walk	yah-gor-do	dern
to eat	or-ja	kin
to sleep	yom-mee-ga	norn

to drink	ar-ga-do	duem
house	yeh	ban
village	kar	moo ban
field	ha	na, rai
water	agah	nam
rice	or	kou
embroidery	gee-gor-der	pakpaa
beautiful	da-ja	suoy
good	da-ja	dee
1	dee-ma	nung
2	nee-ma	sorng
3	seh-ma	sarm
4	or-ma	see
5	mgam-ma	hah
6	cor-ma	hok

SOME USEFUL PHRASES

English	Lahu Shi	Thai
7	sor-ma	jet
8	he-ma	paet
9	gor-ma	kou
10	de-chi	sip
20	de-sow	yee-sip
100	de-roy	nung roy
1000	de-pan	nung pan

WHITE HMONG

English	White Hmong	Thai
hello	nyar djong	sawadee
goodbye	moer jong gor	laa kon, pai la
where are you going?	mo da-gee	pai nai
where are you coming from?	mo da-gee lor	pai nai ma
what is your name?	gor-bey who-lee-ja	chua arai
my name is...	gor-bey who...	chan chua...
I	goo	chan
you	gor	khun
we	o-leng	rou
yes	ehr	krap (kaa for women)
no	gee yua	mai, mai ow
please	tor	chern

SOME USEFUL PHRASES

English	White Hmong	Thai
thank you	woajao	kopkhun
what	da-gee	arai
when	tao-duh	muarai
where	cor-duh	tee-nai
to do	woa	tam
to eat	na-mo	kin
to drink	how-deh	duem
to sleep	mo burr	norn
to walk	mo gay	dern
village	jae	moo ban
house	jae	ban
field	dteh	na, rai
school	jae dao	rong ree-un
car	che	rot

WHITE HMONG

rice	mo	kou
water	deh	nam
embroidery	ban dao	pakpaa
beautiful	yuayong gao	suoy
good	jong	dee
friend	gu-bao	puen
I don't understand	gee bao	chan mai kaojai
never mind / it's nothing	gee or jar	mai benrai
1	ee	nung
2	or	sorng
3	beh	sarm
4	bplow	see
5	gee	hah
6	djow	hok
7	sha-ar	jet

English	White Hmong	Thai
8	yee	paet
9	jawer	kou
10	gow	sip
11	gow-ee	sip-et
12	gow-or	sip-sorng
20	nung gow	yee-sip
100	ea-boo-er	nung roy
1000	ea-zchia	nung pan

LISU

English	Lisu	Thai
hello	a-koe-cha	sawadee
what is your name?	no oh-me-at ma mellay	chua arai
yes	mm	krap (kaa for women)
no	ma nga	mai
please	dee-owe-nee	chern
thankyou	boo moo show	kopkhun
I	mwa	chan
you	nou	khun
we	azo	rou
what	a-shoe-a	arai
where	a-ta	tee-nai
to eat	tza-tza	kin

English	Lisu	Thai
village	a-voo-mur	moo ban
house	he	ban
field	dee-me	na, rai
rice	tza	kou
water	a-de-ar	nam
I don't understand	ma-ser	chan mai koujai
1	tee	nung
2	nee	sorng
3	sa	sarm
4	lee	see
5	mwa	hah
6	tcho	hok
7	shurr	jet

8	hay	paet
9	goo	kou
10	tsue	sip
11	tsue-tee	sip-et
20	nee-tsue	yee-sip
100	tee he-ar	nung roy
1000	tee two	nung pan

PWO KAREN

English	Pwo Karen	Thai
hello	less-oo le	sawadee
goodbye	lee-lon	laa kon, pai la
what is your name?	mine ja low	chua arai
yes	nngh	krap (kaa for women)

SOME USEFUL PHRASES

English	Pwo Karen	Thai
no	lu may be	mai
thank you	nee bow nee-tar	kopkhun
I	yeah	chan
you	plon	khun
we	gu-vay-day	rou
I don't understand	lin a be	chan mai koujai
what	ta-my-le	arai
where	pee-jo-lay	tee-nai
how much	chee do lay	tow-rai
village	doe	moo ban
house	ray	ban
rice	me	kou
water	tee	nam
very good	rree ta	dee mark

1	lu may	nung
2	key may	sorng
3	sa may	sarm
4	lay may	see
5	yeah may	hah
6	choo may	hok
7	no-ay may	jet
8	caw may	paet
9	quee may	kou
10	la chee	sip
11	chee lu may	sip-et
12	chee key may	sip-sorng
20	chee la chee	yee-sip
100	lu ye	nung roy
1000	lu ma	nung pan

While we have changed a few of the names of the interviewees in this book in order to protect their privacy where the interviews were of a highly personal nature, in the case of the vast majority of interviews we have left the names unchanged. It is hoped their openness, coupled with our choice of portraying their lives through this particular medium, will not adversely effect their privacy.

SOURCES

Hilltribe Education Centre, Chiang Rai

Lewis, Paul and Elaine (1984) The Peoples of the Golden Triangle. Thames and Hudson. London.

Population and Community Development Associaton, Chiang Rai Office.